Swindled!

SWINDLED!

CLASSIC BUSINESS FRAUDS
OF THE SEVENTIES

Edited by Donald Moffitt

DOW JONES BOOKS
PRINCETON, NEW JERSEY

Introduction

Jesse D. Quisenberry wore mod suits, high-heeled shoes and a fake Fu Manchu mustache carelessly taped over his lip. To folks in the backcountry Georgia town of Cornelia, he cut quite a figure as he strolled down the main street toting a bag containing hundreds of thousands of dollars in stolen checks that he had cashed at the local bank.

Stanley Goldblum operated in a far more conventional, if parvenuish, milieu. The founder and chief executive of Equity Funding Corporation, he once fired a salesman for selling a ten-year insurance-and-mutual-fund package to an eighty-seven-year-old widow. But under Goldblum's direction, his employees gleefully organized after-hours "parties" at which they fabricated insurance policies on nonexistent people, documented the policies to permit their sale to other insurance companies and then, to collect the payoffs, "killed" the phantom policyholders with phony death claims.

Robert Trippet came from an old and wealthy Oklahoma family. He was a first-class lawyer who didn't really need to press every advantage in every deal he made, but enjoyed doing so anyway. He was one of the first men in the country to capitalize on the appeal of oil drilling as a tax shelter for wealthy individuals, and he organized a company in which they could invest their tax-sheltered dollars. Of the $130 million or so that he raised, $100 million disappeared.

These men were central figures in some of the most creative hanky-panky of recent years. They were diverse in background and personality, and so too were the investors who lost money in their deals. There was Buddy Hackett, for example. The comedian hadn't "the vaguest idea" why he invested $208,000 in Trippet's Home-Stake Production Company. "I just tell jokes," Hackett said. "My lawyer and accountant look into (financial) things and explain them to me in baby talk."

There was Shirley Oakes Butler, daughter of the Bahamas' late Sir Harry Oakes. Mrs. Butler, a politically liberal society woman and a graduate of the Yale law school, was naively persuaded to sell the business enterprises that she and her husband owned. From the buyer, Robert Lee Vesco, they got only $300,000 of the promised $3 million price. Vesco, at the same time, allegedly was looting $224 million from Investors Overseas Services Ltd. (IOS), Bernard Cornfeld's ill-fated mutual-fund venture.

These stories, and others in this book, are told by some of the finest financial investigative reporters in this country: William E. Blundell, Jonathan Kwitny, David McClintick and Stanley Penn, all of the *Wall Street Journal*. While their names may not be household words, these reporters command the respect among their colleagues that, for example, a Bernstein or a Woodward commands among investigative reporters on the political scene.

Penn won a Pulitzer Prize for his reporting on Bahamian politics and financial affairs. Kwitny has written dozens of dazzling newspaper stories and two highly regarded books. And Blundell was the first reporter to discern the imminent collapse of the giant Equity Funding Corporation.

Their craft is a tedious and demanding one, often little understood. But McClintick, in his chapter on the Home-Stake Production case, tells us just how a financial investigative reporter can stumble on and unravel a complicated, massive fraud.

There are lessons to be learned from this book. Corporations with impressive-looking names are no more trustworthy or secure from manipulation than the ordinary human beings who sign and countersign their checks. On the strength of a certified financial statement, a dubious enterprise may raise millions of dollars. It becomes clear, in some of these stories, that blatantly illegal schemes went undiscovered as long as they did, simply because the auditors who certified the financial statements were misled into doing so.

More obvious in some of these pages than in others is the extent to which the public foots the bill for large-scale fraud. It may be in the form of higher prices on the things we buy. As Kwitny points out in his tale of the subornation of the nation's largest meat processor, corruption in the meat business in New York City may add five cents or more per pound to the retail price of beef.

In addition, the public may pay the price in higher taxes. The losses of individual investors or corporations in fraudulent schemes ordinarily are, to some degree, tax-deductible. In the case of Home-Stake Production, the cost to the taxpayer also mounted because many investors turned over their interests in the company to charitable institutions and claimed big tax deductions for well-nigh valueless donations. Whether the government makes up the revenue loss by raising taxes, or failing to lower them when it might otherwise be possible to do so, or borrowing money at interest, makes little practical difference to the taxpayer who pays the bill.

And fraud, even the rarefied high-finance variety, does not weigh just on the Buddy Hacketts or the Shirley Butlers. It is a burden on the poor. Blundell tells of a seventy-four-year-old widow, driven inexorably toward the welfare rolls because she invested $7,000, almost all the money she had, in Equity Funding. And listen to a New Jersey shopkeeper of modest means who lost $25,000, the bulk of his life savings, in the same company. He asked, weeping: "How can I ever tell my wife I lost most of the money we were going to retire on? I don't know what it will do to her, and I'll die of shame."

Throughout the country, institutions that held Equity Funding stock will be paying pensioners a little less, providing less medical care, trimming back student scholarships, financing less research.

That many of the people who manage our corporations

and enforce our laws fail to understand the full implication of all this verges on nonfeasance. Fraud remains a white-collar crime. A man who robs a bank at gunpoint is likely to spend a great part of his life in prison. An embezzler, too, almost surely will be punished harshly, even though his crime involves no threat of violence. By contrast, a New York judge fined Iowa Beef Processors Inc. just $7,000 for paying bribes of $1 million a year to a New York meat broker. The judge said he sympathized with Iowa Beef's chief executive, who had been forced to do what he did to stay in business. The chief executive got off scot-free. The judge said nothing whatsoever about the millions of New York City meat consumers, who were—and today still are—paying for this tribute.

"Society," Blundell writes, "treats the stock swindler with a tolerance that can edge on admiration." Before the bar, he appears as "clearly no surly felon menacing the public safety, but a fellow country-club member who in a moment of weakness strayed from the path and knows it. Give him a light sentence."

But the courts alone should not be expected to police business behavior. Professionals like attorneys and accountants are also responsible for enforcing legal and moral constraints on business. So are managers and corporate directors. Why shouldn't these men simply do the job they are paid to do? This is not an especially revolutionary idea. If anything, it is old-fashioned to the point of quaintness.

Fraud would still go on, as it always has. To understand why, read Blundell. His tale of Equity Funding is one of those real rarities—a moral chiller, a corporate morality epic. It explains a lot.

The Equity Funding fraud never could have succeeded without enlisting the talents and expertise of many otherwise law-abiding people who, for varying reasons, lent their aid and consent to it. One man went along because he believed in "corporate loyalty," whatever that means.

Introduction

Another needed the affection of the older father-figure who led him into crime. Another joined for "the jollies." And another found the fabrication of phony insurance-policy documentation an irresistible challenge to his professionalism

Human motives, all—and because of them we will see corporate fraud again.

Donald Moffitt, Editor

About The Authors

Donald Moffitt, a page-one copy editor for the *Wall Street Journal*, has edited some of the newspaper's major stories on financial scandals. Born in Houston in 1936, he started his newspaper career as a copy boy for the *Houston Post* at the age of sixteen. A Yale graduate, he joined the *Wall Street Journal* in 1960 and worked as a reporter and editor in Dallas, San Francisco and New York. He has won several journalism awards, including Columbia University's Mike Berger Award in 1970, for reporting on New York City affairs. His interest in finance was kindled at the age of eighteen when, although he was under age, he opened a brokerage account and doubled a small stake in the stock market. Though he has never repeated that performance, or even come close to it, he still reads tax cases for fun. His other hobby is fishing, which he pursues almost exclusively in the surf with artificial baits. He is married to Ellen Graham, also a page-one copy editor for the *Wall Street Journal*, and lives in Greenwich Village in New York.

William E. Blundell won the 1974 public service award of the Scripps-Howard Foundation for his coverage of the Equity Funding collapse. Earlier, he had won Columbia University's Mike Berger Award for distinguished New York metropolitan reporting for a *Wall Street Journal* feature story on the Plaza Hotel.

Born forty-one years ago in New York, Blundell attended Syracuse University and served as a U.S. Army missiles officer at Fort Bliss, Texas. Later he did graduate work in journalism and political science at the University of Kansas. He joined the *Wall Street Journal* as a reporter in 1961, later became a page-one editor in New York and now serves as the paper's Los Angeles bureau chief.

Blundell, noted by his colleagues for his dry wit, says he

is "a member of Zeta Psi fraternity, but I forgot the grip and I never send them money, anyway." He hates golf. He and his wife, Gay, live in a Los Angeles suburb, La Canada, which, he asserts, translates from the Spanish as "I've got mine, Jack." He says he likes tennis, hiking, fishing and "watching birds that sit still." He is a senior warden of his Episcopal Church parish. The Blundells have two children.

Jonathan Kwitny is one of the *Wall Street Journal's* most energetic staffers. His working day begins at 4:00 A.M. and often doesn't end until late at night. Such a schedule has permitted Kwitny to write two highly regarded nonfiction books while working full-time at the paper. His books are "The Fountain Pen Conspiracy" (Alfred A. Knopf, 1973) and "The Mullendore Murder Case" (Farrar, Straus and Giroux, 1974). He is currently working on a novel.

Born in 1941 in Indianapolis, Kwitny became editor of the *Shortridge Daily Echo*, the oldest and largest high school daily anywhere. He graduated from the University of Missouri and received a master's degree in history from New York University. Before joining the *Wall Street Journal* in 1971, he worked as a reporter for local newspapers in New Jersey and New York and twice won first prize for distinguished public service from the New Jersey Press Association. He interrupted his newspaper career for two years to serve as a Peace Corps volunteer, teaching secondary-school English and literature in Nigeria.

Kwitny's wife, Martha, is a lawyer and state prosecutor in New Jersey.

David McClintick has written many *Wall Street Journal* stories on securities and tax fraud and on the Internal Revenue Service. Among them: how former House Ways and Means Committee Chairman Wilbur Mills pressured the IRS into granting a $100 million tax concession to several big shoe companies; how International Telephone and Telegraph Corporation's acquisition of Hartford Fire Insurance Company was made possible by an IRS ruling that

ITT obtained under questionable circumstances, and how the IRS occasionally administers federal tax laws unevenly, unfairly and unconstitutionally.

Born in Kansas, McClintick went to high school in Montana, graduated from Harvard and earned a master's degree in journalism at Columbia. He served as a U.S. Army intelligence officer in Japan, the Philippines, Vietnam and Washington, D.C. He enjoys music. His wife, Judith, is a musician and faculty member at Columbia's Teachers College.

McClintick is writing a book on the Home-Stake tax-shelter case to be published by M. Evans and Company.

Stanley Penn, for twenty-three years a *Wall Street Journal* reporter, shared with Monroe W. Karmin a Pulitzer Prize for national reporting in 1967. Penn and Karmin won the prize for a series of articles exposing the roles of casino gambling and conflicts of interest in Bahamian political and business affairs. The series also earned them the 1967 distinguished service award of Sigma Delta Chi, the professional journalism fraternity. And also in 1967, Penn was among a group of *Wall Street Journal* reporters to win a G. M. Loeb Award, sponsored by the University of Connecticut, for a series of articles on classic corporate rivalries.

Penn, forty-seven years old, was born in New York City. He graduated from the University of Missouri. He lives with his wife, Esther, and their two children on Manhattan's West Side.

Contents

I

The Quisenberry Caper

By Jonathan Kwitny

This is a tale of two cities:

Boston, with its patrician financial institutions and its North End underworld, right out of a George V. Higgins novel, where shadowy FBI informants double-cross flashy gangsters who bar-hop in chauffeured limousines, hand out thick packets of fresh banknotes and die in real shoot-outs.

And Cornelia, in the Georgia hill country of the novel and movie, *Deliverance*, where small-town bankers, who didn't go to Harvard, command the modest deposits of small farmers and townsfolk for whom the most familiar law-enforcement officer may be the local game ranger or the federal whiskey revenuer.

Somehow, in 1971, more than 1.1 million patrician dollars from Boston made their way to one of Cornelia's backcountry bankers. The money then went to a fellow who called himself Jesse D. Quisenberry. People noticed that Jesse D. Quisenberry was a little odd. For one thing, he had trouble keeping his Fu Manchu mustache in place. For another, he used a cloth bag to lug away down Cornelia's main street, in broad daylight, huge bundles of small-denomination bills. These bills had been trucked up especially from the Federal Reserve Bank in Atlanta and used by the local bank to cash his checks.

The story also involves a quiet, $22,000-a-year New England accountant and family man who suddenly owns a new

1

Continental Mark IV, moves to Las Vegas, buys an $85,000 house and begins running sex shows in casinos. Then there is the gunshot killing of two men in a feud over a honey-blonde neurosurgeon who operates in prominent hospitals. And a bizarre arson in an office building. A game ranger from a family with moonshining and banking connections. And a hit-and-run accident—involving a boat.

Since 1971, no positive trace of the main character, Jesse D. Quisenberry, has been found. Some people think he successfully pulled off, with a few accomplices, one of the slickest thefts in history and now is living quite well somewhere. On the other hand, Robert Smith, the assistant U.S. attorney who vainly tried to prosecute the case, thinks Quisenberry isn't living at all. Instead, he says, Quisenberry drew too slow in a pistol fight in Boston several months after the money grab.

One thing is sure. The stolen $1.1 million still is missing. And Aetna Casualty and Surety Company, which bonded the financial institutions in Boston, is slugging it out in court with Lumbermens Mutual Casualty Company, which bonded the country bank in Cornelia, Georgia. The insurance dispute is being fought in the U.S. District Court in Atlanta. The outcome will determine who has to make up the cash that Jesse D. Quisenberry took.

It is not the kind of case that hits the federal courts every day.

The story told here has been pieced together from thousands of pages of sworn depositions and other records filed in the insurance dispute and from dozens of interviews. It begins on October 20 1971, in the office of Roderick A. Munroe, financial vice president of Perini Corporation, the big construction firm based in the Boston suburb of Framingham. The telephone rings. It is Brown Brothers, Harriman and Company, the private bankers, reporting that Perini's checking account is substantially overdrawn. Never before in his twenty-five years at Perini has Munroe heard of such a thing.

For several months, Munroe has been suffering from a nervous condition that later forces him to take a prolonged leave of absence. His condition isn't helped on October 20 when his secretary, Jill Valle, follows up the phone call. She can't reconcile the latest banking statement from Brown Brothers, which has been lying around since it arrived October 7. Canceled checks accounting for more than $750,000 in charges against Perini's account seem to be missing from the envelope containing the statement.

Munroe and Mrs. Valle are still trying to figure this out the next day when a call comes from Perini's other blue blood bankers, Morgan Guaranty Trust Company. This Perini account, too, is substantially overdrawn.

Mrs. Valle reminds Munroe that the entire Morgan statement—checks and all—disappeared from her filing cabinet not long after it arrived October 7. She remembers the date very well because the next morning, October 8, she arrived at work to find that her office had been fire-bombed, along with much of the rest of the Perini financial department's office.

According to Detective Sgt. Thomas S. Cobb, who investigated the bombing for the Framingham police department, birthday candles had been stuck on coverless matchbooks atop gasoline-filled plastic bags and lighted. He knew this because some candles had fizzled, leaving some devices intact. Cobb noted also that the sabotage took place between 5:45 A.M., when the nightwatchman normally completed his rounds, and 7 A.M., when the first employees normally arrived—and that there were no signs of forcible entry.

"My feeling was that it was not the work of a professional," Cobb said. For one thing, the bombs were placed where the automatic sprinkler system could douse them quickly. "A professional would have been aware of the sprinkler system," the sergeant said. "He could have easily turned it off." Later, after the check swindle was discovered, investigators theorized that the firebombs weren't intended to cause much damage, but were planted to disguise the theft of canceled checks, vouchers and other documents. Though many documents were missing afterward, few in the office were found burned.

On October 21, Munroe asked Morgan Guaranty and Brown Brothers for an accounting of the missing checks. The banks found photocopies and reported back that seventeen checks, totaling $1,129,232.29, bore preprinted numbers that were out of sequence with the numbers on the rest of the Perini checks that the banks cleared in September.

On hearing this, Munroe and his second in command, chief accountant Roland A. Kinsley, made their way to the storeroom where Perini kept its supply of unused checks. Getting there was easy enough. The checks were kept in the same unlocked room where Perini stocked styrofoam coffee cups. Every clerk and secretary was used to walking right in. A quick inventory by Munroe and Kinsley showed that someone also had walked right out again carrying one box of prenumbered checks on the Morgan Guaranty account and one box of prenumbered checks on the Brown Brothers account. The numbers on the missing checks matched the numbers of the out-of-sequence checks cashed by the banks.

A complete accounting showed that the cashed checks were almost evenly divided between the two banks and carried dates between September 3 and September 22. Because Perini kept large bank balances, it took almost a month of additional check writing before the accounts ran into the red. The checks were made payable to two construction firms Perini had never done business with, and were endorsed by one Jesse D. Quisenberry, of whom no one at Perini admitted knowledge. They were cashed at First National Bank of Habersham County, Georgia.

The checks appeared to have been written on the financial department's checkwriting machine, which automatically signed Munroe's name to spare him writer's cramp every month. The banks had been told to accept the machine signature. A manager for Burroughs Corporation, which makes the machine, testified that "We tout it as the ultimate in check protection and control. Its sole purpose in a customer's office is to afford the highest degree of protection against check fraud."

Despite warnings from its corporate auditors, Arthur Andersen and Company, Perini had found it inconvenient to use certain control procedures. For example: The machine dumped signed checks into a box that was supposed to be locked; the key was supposed to be kept by an employee of a different department. No such employee had been assigned, however, and the box was unlocked. Nor did anyone pay any attention to the machine's counter, which kept track of the number of checks written so that the number on any day could be compared with the number of vouchers authorized for payment that day.

All this, Kinsley said later in a deposition, was "too much trouble."

To make the unauthorized checks look legitimate, whoever prepared them typed on them numbers similar to real voucher numbers Perini used at the time. This suggested that the schemers had inside knowledge of company accounting procedures. Whoever prepared the checks, too, apparently knew that Perini's balances at a third bank were temporarily low. No checks were drawn on this account.

Many employees in the financial department know all this. But only three persons had keys to the checkwriting machine: Munroe, Kinsley and Charles Bamforth, third in command of the financial department. Of those three, only Munroe and Kinsley had keys to the office building so they could enter at odd hours.

Kinsley later remembered that, at one point, Munroe "told me that he had thought it over and it had to be either him or me and that he knew it was not him. My response to that was, 'Well, I know it was not me, so where does that leave us?' "

Meanwhile, another question was in everyone's mind at Perini: What, and where, was the First National Bank of Habersham County, Georgia?

Across from the First National Bank of Habersham County, dominating the main intersection of Cornelia, Georgia, is a twenty-foot statue of an apple, painted bright red. Habersham County calls itself "The Home of the Big Red Apple." Founded in 1909, the bank was taken over in 1928 by the late F. M. Reeves. His son, Lewis, dropped out of the tenth grade to become a janitor at the bank. Eventually, Lewis Reeves laid aside his mop and journeyed up Highway 23 to Clarksville, the county seat, to work. Later he opened a hardware store in nearby Clayton. Reeves Hardware—now really a variety store—has become the Macy's of Clayton.

In 1964, when he was eighty-seven, F. M. Reeves decided he needed an understudy to succeed him as banker. So son Lewis left the store, became vice president of the bank and, a year later, when his father retired, took over as president. His sister, Elizabeth Reeves Kimzey, who had joined the bank in 1930, remained vice president and cashier.

At the beginning of 1971, the bank's total resources had reached $18 million.

Reeves and Mrs. Kimzey have sworn in depositions that the first time they ever saw or heard of Jesse D. Quisenberry was on September 7, 1971, when he walked in unannounced and asked to see the president about opening an account. For the next twenty-four days, he was a customer of the bank.

Quisenberry cut quite a figure among the overalled farmers of Cornelia with his mod suits, loud ties, chrome-rimmed glasses, high-heeled shoes, long hair and Fu Manchu mustache. Reeves said he paid little attention to the Fu Manchu because "I don't believe in mustaches." But to

6

Billy Ray Loudermilk, the bank's collections manager, the mustache clearly was phony.

"I looked down, you know, and I noticed you could see like a Band-Aid-looking tape right around the edge of one side," Loudermilk later said. "And I laughed to myself, 'Well, that son of a gun. . . . I would like to buy me some sideburns (like that) because I can't grow them.' I know he knew I noticed it because I bugged my eyes out at him."

Quisenberry's accent also drew wide notice. "He doesn't talk Southern like I do," Loudermilk said. To Reeves, "He didn't have our ole Southern drawl . . . but it wasn't a Boston accent as we hear the Kennedys and those boys talk."

Somehow, Quisenberry and Reeves hit it off.

Bank employees and others gossiped about Quisenberry's peculiar appearance. Reeves ignored the talk. To speak to Reeves about Quisenberry was "sort of like . . . talking to a wall," one vice president testified. When Loudermilk and another employee were laughing about the mustache, Reeves walked up, according to Loudermilk, and asked, "What the hell's so funny?" When he was told, he walked icily off.

Reeves said that in ten or fifteen minutes on his first visit to the bank, Quisenberry asked to open an account, filled out application cards and deposited three checks from Perini Corporation, drawn on its Brown Brothers account, payable to Quisenberry Contracting Company. The checks, dated September 3, came to $195,861.12. Quisenberry's personalized checks for his new account were printed on the spot, and he left with them.

Reeves said he didn't ask his new customer many questions, and Quisenberry didn't provide much information; he didn't state his business, and he offered no identification. Months later, when the FBI looked up the Atlanta address that Quisenberry had given the bank, agents found a vacant lot.

On September 10, Quisenberry deposited two checks dated September 7. On September 15, he deposited three checks dated September 9. Nobody ever asked why Perini would issue him several checks for varying amounts on the same date.

Mrs. Kimzey testified that in her forty years at the bank, perhaps five customers had accounts of more than $250,000. But she routinely, without question, submitted Quisenberry's first half-million-dollars of checks to Fulton National Bank in Atlanta, First National's city correspondent, for payment. They were cleared through Brown Brothers.

On September 16, after the first three had cleared, Quisenberry withdrew $195,707.90 in cash. As the later checks were cleared, he kept on withdrawing. On September 18, he opened a new account for Southern Contracting Company with Perini checks drawn on Morgan Guaranty.

He dealt only with Reeves and his sister, Mrs. Kimzey. They said they assumed that Quisenberry was proprietor of the companies whose checks he deposited. "I asked him if it (one of the companies) was a corporation," Mrs. Kimzey said, "and he told me it was a plain company. . . . That's the reason I used the plain (application) card."

Other hands at the bank were used to deferring to the management methods of Reeves and Mrs. Kimzey. George Pierce Short Jr., a retired Army colonel, had gone to work for the bank as a vice president in 1970 and tried to establish standard account-handling procedures like those used by bigger banks. But in a deposition in 1974 he said, "It became obvious to me that Mr. Reeves or Mrs. Kimzey had no desire, no intention to allow any paper or guide . . . to change those methods of operation . . . which in most cases were known only to themselves." Shortly after the deposition, Colonel Short was fired.

Claud Surface, another vice president asked for a credit check on Quisenberry on September 17 from the Fulton National Bank. Three days later, the Atlanta bank phoned that it could find no record of Quisenberry or his companies. Surface passed the news on to Reeves, but the bank continued cashing its new customer's checks.

Curious, Colonel Short and Loudermilk buttonholed Quisenberry in the bank lobby on occasion but found him uncommunicative. Colonel Short recalls: "I got the impression that Quisenberry . . . possibly was interested in constructing a motel" near Cornelia. "I think that our conversation was more about the weather and the climate here in the north Georgia area, perhaps, as opposed to that in Florida, I think. I don't remember that Mr. Quisenberry had very much to say."

Mrs. Kimzey, according to depositions, was always ready with Quisenberry's enormous currency needs when he came to cash his checks, although sometimes it would take her fifteen minutes or so to count out the small bills. Sometimes, before or after his visits, she had to phone the Federal Reserve Bank in Atlanta to rush hundreds of thousands of dollars to Cornelia by armored car. At least once, his check cashing reduced the bank's cash reserve below the legal minimum.

Lynn Jordan, a teller, remembered that once when Mrs. Kimzey didn't have as many $20 bills in the bank vault as Quisenberry wanted, she borrowed some from the tellers.

Quisenberry usually hauled off his loot in a black briefcase. But once it wouldn't fit and he had to borrow a cloth bag to carry it, too.

The last week in September, First National mailed Quisenberry his monthly statement. It came back from the Atlanta post office marked "No known addressee." Mrs. Kimzey said that she told Quisenberry about it on his next visit and that he said he would pick up his statements in person. On October 1, he cashed a final check for $220,000, leaving $1,156.30 in his two accounts, and told Mrs. Kimzey he wouldn't be back. He wasn't. She later said she asked no questions.

Afterward, she and Reeves did find a use for some of the Perini money Quisenberry had left behind. They charged the balance of the accounts $500 for the trouble he had caused by making it necessary for money to be trucked in from the Fed, and another $46 to cover the fine imposed on the little bank for letting its cash reserve get too low.

When Perini discovered its $1.1 million loss in October, the company immediately reported it to the FBI. The bureau assigned agent Robert E. Sheehan to investigate.

According to Assistant U.S. Attorney Jerry O'Sullivan, who supervised the investigation in Boston, Sheehan is "the best FBI agent in the country" because of his encyclopedic knowledge of criminals and their modes of operation.

David Perini was general counsel of Perini Corporation. He and other Perini officials met with Sheehan to recount how more than $1.1 million in unauthorized checks had been run through the Perini check-writing machine and cashed in September at the rural First National Bank of Habersham County.

When he had heard the story, Sheehan replied: "There is only one guy in Boston capable of this . . . and that's Mickey Morrissey."

"If you know a character like that," David Perini asked the supersleuth, "why isn't he in jail?"

Michael Morrissey, then thirty-five years old, had been in jail. In the 1950s he was convicted and imprisoned for armed robbery of a bank, and in the mid-1960s, for receiving stolen property—checks used in a $45,000 bank swindle. Federal authorities say he would have gone to prison a third time, for a $300,000 caper in 1970, but for the intervention of a Massachusetts politician.

According to the authorities, Morrissey had charmed himself into the graces of a state bank examiner and persuaded him to smuggle out checks printed for big customers from the banks he was examining. Then Morrissey made offset copies of the checks and, according to the authorities, cashed them at branch banks using forged signatures. He is believed to have bilked six banks of $50,000 each. The case never was prosecuted.

If Michael Morrissey masterminded the Perini scheme, Sheehan decided, he must have had inside help again. So the agent borrowed photographs of Perini executives and began showing them to FBI informants in the Boston underworld. Almost immediately, one Perini man was identified as a frequent luncheon companion of Morrissey's in the summer of 1971. Usually they ate at Polcari's, a North End restaurant, and sometimes also at the Boston Playboy Club. The official was Roland A. Kinsley, Perini's chief accountant and, according to sworn depositions, one of only two men who had keys both to Perini's check-writing machine and to the Perini office building in suburban Framingham.

Agent Sheehan took this information to Perini executives. Charles J. Patterson, vice president for corporate relations, recalled the occasion. "Mr. Perini (the late Louis Perini, then chairman) said to the FBI man, 'You know, we don't really know this fellow (Kinsley) very well.' And this bothered me a little bit, since I was in charge of employee relations, so I said, 'Well, I think we know him, Mr. Perini, but he is a very quiet fellow.'"

Indeed, the forty-two-year-old Kinsley had lived his entire life in the town of his birth, Minden, Massachusetts, which Patterson described as "a very out-of-the-way place. It's not the kind of town you would ever visit or go through on the way to any place." Kinsley was a graduate of a local junior college, married and the father of three teen-agers. For ten years, he had been the Minden town treasurer.

In a 1973 deposition, Kinsley recalled how he met Morrissey. Kinsley was looking in on a Perini construction project near Polcari's restaurant and stopped for lunch. "This restaurant is more or less a meeting part of Boston," he said. "Judges, doctors, anybody you name was probably in there. I was in a group sitting there, eating, and Mr.

Swindled!

Morrissey came over and sat down, and somebody said, 'This is Mr. Morrissey.' He evidently knew everybody else at the table. . . . He was a great talker—a heck of a nice guy."

Kinsley said that Morrissey knew without asking that he worked for Perini. "I had no idea what he (Morrissey) did," Kinsley said. "When I first met him, he said something about being a doctor, but somebody said he is only kidding, he likes to pass himself off as a doctor." (A woman acquaintance, however, testified that she met Morrissey in a restaurant too, and that when she asked his occupation, "he said he was a professional thief.")

Kinsley and Morrissey met a number of times for lunch. Kinsley testified that he couldn't remember what they talked about at their frequent two-hour luncheons. "It was generally just conversation," he said. He did remember that Chester Poliskey—known to law-enforcement officials as Morrissey's bodyguard—would hang around the restaurant during lunch. "He wouldn't sit down. . . . I never heard him say a word," Kinsley recalled.

Perini officials heard agent Sheehan out and debated what to do. The evidence against Kinsley, they decided, was too circumstantial to justify firing him right off. They did abandon the check-writing machine and excluded him from those authorized to write checks by hand.

Meanwhile, investigators began checking up again on Morrissey. Eventually they found Ann Powell, a Scituate, Massachusetts, real-estate saleswoman, who said Morrissey had visited her several times beginning in the late summer of 1971 to inquire about ocean-front "mini-estates."

"I told him that nice, good places on the waterfront come very expensive, anywhere from $350,000 to $500,000," Mrs. Powell testified. "It didn't faze him. . . . He wanted something real posh. . . . He told me that he was with the Teamsters union in an official capacity, so I thought maybe there was a little hanky-panky."

One evening Mrs. Powell joined Morrissey and his fiance, Carolyn Sukus, for dinner. She said they picked her up in a chauffeur-driven Cadillac. Another time, she went with the couple in the limousine to see television star Dave Garroway's home, which was for sale, only a few blocks from the Perini family home. Morrissey made a bid, but it was rejected. Rather than bid the price higher, he agreed to rent it. He handed over his first payment, $2,000, "in a paper bag that he slipped out of his inside coat pocket," Mrs. Powell testified.

The money was in $20 bills, she said, bound in tape as if it had just come from a bank.

Morrissey paid his rent for November 1971, but the December payment never arrived.

On December 31, Mrs. Powell telephoned Miss Sukus to ask about it.

She was told that Morrissey had "died accidentally."

Morrissey had died, though hardly accidentally. Back in 1965, Morrissey, then divorced from his first wife and working as a drugstore clerk, had married Shirley Otis, a honey-blonde twenty-nine-year old graduate of Tufts medical school who practiced neurology at St. Elizabeth's Hospital in Boston. Later Morrissey worked as a truck driver, a construction worker, a nightclub manager and a delicatessen operator while Dr. Otis moved up to the more prestigious Beth Israel Hospital.

Morrissey and Dr. Otis had two children. But they argued because, in her words, "he always had money. . . . I assumed he wasn't making money in a legal way." In 1968, as he prepared to go to prison for the second time, they separated. They were divorced in 1970. Meanwhile, Dr. Otis continued to see Morrissey after his release from prison in 1970, usually when he visited their children.

Dr. Otis began dating Robert Carr, a truck driver. Morrissey found out, Dr. Otis testified, and expressed "strong feelings that he didn't want me to date anyone, period. It was more or less a threat."

13

Swindled!

On Thanksgiving night, 1971, Morrissey saw Carr's automobile parked at Dr. Otis' house. She was giving a Thanksgiving dinner. She said Morrissey "stopped and tried to break down the door . . . threatened to kill . . . went home and got a gun. And we called the police. I guess he saw the police," she said, because he didn't come back that night. Afraid, Carr got a pistol for his home. Later, Morrissey bragged to Dr. Otis that he had broken into Carr's apartment, talked to his former wife and had him followed.

On Christmas night, Dr. Otis again had Carr and relatives for dinner. Again, Morrissey stopped by. He "walked in the house and spotted Bob and went over to him and said, 'You're a dead man,' " Dr. Otis testified.

Carr testified that he went home and went to sleep. "I was awakened by the sound of glass shattering and my bedroom door was opened," he said. "I saw two men approaching my bedroom silhouetted against some sort of a back light coming from the street, or the moon. . . . And I just knew that they were coming to kill me. . . . There were shots exchanged and a terrific amount of physical fighting. . . . They hit me with a crowbar over the head and I received numerous. . . wounds. . . . I shot at them both and they shot at me. . . . And so I killed them." One of the men later was identified as Morrissey.

Carr had bullets in both his legs. At a hospital, asked by police and reporters whether Morrissey was involved in the Perini theft, Carr responded that Morrissey had bragged about it. Later, in 1974, Carr would retract this, saying he had "perhaps exaggerated" the tale because he had thought the men he shot were hired killers and he didn't know that Morrissey was dead. He said he wanted "to make sure that Morrissey gets put in jail, or he'll try to kill me in the hospital. . . . I was in terror, and I tell you that you would be, too."

The other corpse in Carr's apartment was that of Chester Poliskey, Morrissey's bodyguard.

Even before the shooting, FBI agents from Atlanta had

14

shown photographs of Morrissey and Poliskey to employees of the First National Bank of Habersham County. Several said that Poliskey resembled Jesse D. Quisenberry. Although none could make a positive identification, it was enough to persuade Robert Smith, an assistant U.S. attorney in Atlanta, that Poliskey was Quisenberry. However, an insurance lawyer who is deeply involved in the case says Smith "is the only one who believes that."

In any event, investigators had begun trying to link Morrissey with the Georgia bank.

Two Eastern Airlines stewardesses tentatively identified Morrissey's photo as that of a man who traveled from Boston to Atlanta in September. Checks of airline and rental car records didn't prove fruitful, but combing the telephone records of Morrissey's women friends did. Aside from his limousine companionship with Miss Sukus and his jealous attentions to Dr. Otis, he had become the only man ever to receive a key to the Boston apartment of a Northeast Airlines stewardess, according to what she told authorities. In September 1971, investigators found that several telephone calls were made from her apartment to the Royal Coach Inn on Atlanta's north side. The stewardess said she didn't make the calls. The motel's guest-registration cards, inspected by a reporter, turned up no clue to whoever was being called.

Neither did the stewardess make two other possibly significant phone calls, both dialed from her apartment on September 13 1971, to 778–2876 in Cornelia, Georgia. That was the number of the direct line to the office of Lewis Reeves, who was president of the First National Bank of Habersham County. Reeves, however, tells a reporter, "I never got no damned calls. I'm not going to tell you a damned thing. You're just too damned inquisitive."

Investigators were intrigued by another telephone call, made in August 1971 from a motel outside Atlanta to Morrissey's home in Boston. The motel room was occupied at the time by Harry Henry Sitner, a seventy-six-year old gambler and convicted confidence man who had just been released from federal prison after serving a term for transporting stolen jewelry in New England. Some time before his death in 1974, Sitner told authorities that a guest in his motel room, Garland "Bud" Cochran, a convicted moonshiner from Elijay, Georgia, had made the call to Morrissey.

Sitner and Cochran (the latter now a fugitive on a drug-smuggling indictment) had met in the federal prison at Eglin Air Force Base, Florida. Cochran was well-known around the First National Bank of Habersham County. At the time of the Perini theft, he had an outstanding loan at the bank. But Sitner was unwilling or unable to tell authorities how or why Cochran happened to phone Morrissey.

Then, about the time Morrissey was killed, the case seemed about to break.

Colonel Short, then still a vice president of the Cornelia bank, attended a party in late 1971 at the home of Clyde Dixon, executive vice president of the Peoples Bank in Cleveland, Georgia, near Cornelia. Conversation turned to the Perini theft. ("Everybody in Cornelia, talked about the Quisenberry thing," another bank officer recalls. "They still do. You know, we never had anything to talk about before.")

Colonel Short was stunned when Dixon said that he had been offered $50,000 or 5 percent of the gross, as a personal fee to cash without question about $1 million in checks for a stranger. Dixon said the offer was delivered by W. L. "Dub" Lovell, a game ranger, one of seven brothers, of whom four have been convicted of federal tax violations involving moonshine. Dub Lovell, however, never has been convicted of a crime.

Not long afterward, Colonel Short got another jolt. On a visit to the Habersham Bank of Clarksville, Georgia, he heard a similar story from Tom Arrandale, chairman of the bank. In this case, however, the offer supposedly came from Dub Lovell's brother, Carlos Lovell, who had pleaded guilty to a moonshining charge in 1949 and who had been acquitted in a 1962 moonshining case in which a third brother, Fred Lovell, was convicted.

When an attempt was made to interview him for this story, Carlos Lovell refused to talk about it. "You better just put your suitcase back in that rig (a rented Pinto) and go back where you came from," he said. "I'm not gonna tell you nothin'."

Though moonshining may not get you into north Georgia's fanciest country clubs, it is an accepted livelihood, and the Lovells are no strangers to legitimate business. One brother, Earl, was a real-estate partner of Lewis Reeves. Dub Lovell also had met Reeves.

Their encounter came one evening in August 1961. J. H. Wilson, an Atlanta real-estate man, was taking friends for a boat ride near his summer home at Lake Burton in Rabun County, just north of Habersham County. Wilson says that he was pulling away from his dock when a powerful Chris Craft without lights smashed into his boat and sped away. He and a passenger were badly injured and spent several weeks in the hospital.

Dub Lovell, game ranger, investigated the accident. His search for a Chris Craft with a damaged bow ended at Lewis Reeves' dock. Reeves denied any blame for the accident and according to his deposition and records in the county court, he wasn't charged with a crime.

Colonel Short testified that shortly after the Quisenberry affair, Dub Lovell began banking at Reeve's First National Bank of Habersham County and often appeared there. Colonel Short also told the FBI what the other bankers had told him about Dub and Carlos Lovell.

A federal grand jury in Atlanta subpoenaed Dub Lovell in 1971. He denied proposing the check-cashing scheme to Dixon. Dub Lovell was indicted for perjury. At the October 1972 trial, Dixon testified against him. On cross examination, it was revealed that Dixon had a drinking problem; that he was a member of the state game and fish commission; that Dub Lovell had long been assigned as his driver and that the two men had quarreled on occasion. Evidence about the Perini swindle and the alleged offer to Arrandale by Lovell's brother was ruled inadmissible. The jury acquitted Dub Lovell.

Since then, the investigation has sputtered. FBI agents still cull occasional leads, but the clock on the five-year-statute of limitations is rapidly ticking away. In Georgia, banker Arrandale has received anonymous telephone threats to his and his son's lives. Banker Dixon has hired an armed guard to protect his property; vandals have broken into it twice, anyway.

Perini executives have become disenchanted with the FBI's efforts. David Perini, the general counsel, testified in 1973, "They would tell us things like, 'We think we are ready to go to the grand jury on this,' and, you know, everything was just around the corner, but then it never happened."

Shortly after Morrissey was shot dead, Perini fired Roland Kinsley, the chief accountant, solely on the ground that he had met often with Morrissey before the theft. The same day, Perini hired a private investigator to tail him. The private eye did observe Kinsley cruising around in a new Continental Mark IV. Otherwise, he found Kinsley's routine extremely routine, and he gave up the tail job.

Within a few months, Kinsley had taken off for Las Vegas, where he had gambled a few times before on tours. He testified that he stayed for a while free of charge at the Thunderbird. He broke his ankle in a culvert on the property, he said, "and I think possibly they were afraid of a large lawsuit." He testified that he paid $15,000 down on an $85,000 house and began managing "a sex show" at the Gay 90s and later at the Royal Las Vegas Hotel. Since then, both shows have closed and Kinsley can't be reached; he has no phone listing in Las Vegas. He never was charged with any offense.

Banker Reeves retired from the Cornelia bank and sold most of his stock in it. He still runs Reeves Hardware in Clayton. He has sworn in a deposition that he didn't make a cent in the Quisenberry affair.

Dr. Shirley Otis married Robert Carr, who still suffers from the gunshot wounds in his legs. As of the summer of 1974, Carr was keeping house for the couple in Del Mar, California. Dr. Otis was practicing at the highly regarded Scripps Clinic and Research Foundation at La Jolla. Carol Sukus, who married Morrissey in Las Vegas shortly before he died, has moved from Massachusetts.

What happened to the money remains a mystery.

Aetna Casualty had insured Perini for up to $1 million against theft. Four banks had handled Perini's stolen checks. Aetna and Perini had to decide whom to sue to recover. Under standard insurance-industry procedure, the suit would be filed in Perini's name; but Aetna, which had paid Perini $1 million, would run the legal show and pay the bills.

Perini wanted to keep its friendly relations with Brown Brothers, Harriman and Morgan Guaranty, the banks where it kept the accounts on which the stolen checks were drawn. It encouraged these two banks to team up as plaintiffs with Perini against the two Georgia banks—the First National Bank of Habersham County, which had cashed the stolen checks, and its correspondent, Fulton National Bank in Atlanta. If Brown Brothers and Morgan Guaranty wouldn't join the suit as plaintiffs, Perini would have to sue them as defendants.

Brown Brothers decided to become a plaintiff, and Aetna approved. Morgan Guaranty, on the other hand, threw in with Fulton National, a major customer, and became a defendant in the suit. Running the defense is Lumbermens Mutual Casualty, which had insured the Cornelia bank in

1971. (It stopped insuring the bank after the Quisenberry affair.)

In the summer of 1975, U.S. District Judge Albert Henderson in Atlanta ordered Morgan Guaranty and Fulton National dismissed as defendants, leaving First National Bank of Habersham County still a defendant. But the plaintiffs appealed the dismissals to the U.S. Circuit Court of Appeals, which was scheduled to hear arguments on the issue in the fall.

The defense contends that Perini failed to take adequate precautions in writing checks and that the Quisenberry checks were cleared according to Perini's standing instructions, so that the Georgia banks and Morgan Guaranty had no reason not to honor them.

David Perini sums up Perini's attitude: "You know," he testified, "I live in Framingham and if I had a check for $100 drawn on another bank and then went down to the Framingham Trust Company to cash it—and we do business with the Framingham Trust Company—chances are they would probably check it. . . . The idea that someone can put more than $1 million worth of checks through . . . a small bank without anyone making any attempt to check whether the payee is in existence, to call the company upon whom those checks were drawn . . . is absolutely inconceivable to me."

But it's just what happened.

II

How Vesco Took a Jet-Set Couple for a Ride

By Stanley Penn

Allan Butler and his wife, Shirley Oakes Butler, belong to Nassau society. Butler, forty-nine, was born in Cambridge, Massachusetts, and graduated from Harvard with a bachelor of science degree. He got his master's at Johns Hopkins. For a while, he published a small New Hampshire newspaper. Then he gave it up to become a European representative of First National Bank of Boston. Later he joined Fairbanks, Morse and Company, a Chicago industrial concern, as financial vice president.

Shirley Butler, a Yale law school graduate, was the daughter of Sir Harry Oakes, an American-born prospector who made a fortune from a gold strike in Canada and retired to live in splendor in Nassau, capital of the Bahamas. Sir Harry's murder in 1943 was a worldwide press sensation. It was never solved.

The Butlers were married in 1961. Shortly after, aided by some of the money that Mrs. Butler inherited from Sir Harry, the couple started a merchant (or commercial) bank in a small pink building on Charlotte Street in downtown Nassau. Butlers Bank invested for its own account, handled trust funds for wealthy customers and made loans. The bank, of which Allan Butler became chairman, was only a short walk from "Jacaranda," the Butlers' elegant home, complete with servants, a swimming pool and tennis court. Politically liberal, the Butlers were among the first of their set openly to support Lynden Pindling, the Bahamas' first black prime minister, who came to power in 1967. His Progressive Liberal Party had won a close election from the "Bay Street Boys," white merchant-politicians who had long been entrenched in government.

The Butlers, in all likelihood, would have enjoyed a quiet, uneventful life had they not become involved with Robert Lee Vesco. Then an obscure New Jersey industrialist, Vesco later was to gain international notoriety. He was accused by the U.S. Securities and Exchange Commission of master-minding one of the largest securities frauds on record. As a result of his dealings with the Butlers, Vesco was able to gain control of International Overseas Services Ltd. (IOS), a giant mutual-fund company, founded in 1956 by the flamboyant Bernard Cornfeld. IOS at one time controlled assets of more than $2 billion. The Butlers have suffered from their association with Vesco and IOS.

Butler's reputation has been tarnished. He was named as one of forty-two individual and corporate defendants in a massive civil suit brought by the SEC in November 1972, charging Vesco and his colleagues with the misappropriation of $224 million from four investor-owned mutual funds managed by IOS.

Butler lost more than just his dignity. Vesco, abetted by his chief associate, Norman LeBlanc, managed to divest the Butlers of Lewis-Oakes Ltd., a Bahamian holding company owned by Shirley Butler. In exchange for its assets, the Butlers received only a fraction of the payment they say they were promised under the written agreement.

Among the assets obtained by the Vesco group were Butlers Bank; the controlling block of stock in a Toronto company, Security Capital Corporation, which at the time had interests in nursing homes, a gold mine and an office-supplies distributor; a control block of stock in General Bahamian Companies, operator of a retail liquor-wine chain, drug stores, a large auto distributorship and a computer service bureau; and Charlotte Street Properties, which owned Charlotte House, a modern office building, and a profitable parking lot, both in downtown Nassau. For these assets, the Butlers maintain, they were promised $3 million in cash over a three-year period. Instead, they say, they got $300,000, or 10 percent of the purchase price, with no likelihood at all of getting the balance. Vesco and Le-Blanc disclaim any financial obligation to the Butlers.

The Butlers considered themselves blatantly swindled. They sued in Bahamas Supreme Court to get the money they say is owed them, or failing that, to recover the assets they turned over to Vesco-LeBlanc. A receiver appointed by the court has been attempting to get back the assets in question since 1974.

But, as the long-persevering receiver has discovered, it is no simple task. The various assets of Lewis-Oakes Ltd. were squirreled away by Vesco-LeBlanc through a maze of shell companies—corporate entities with no assets. The couple's efforts to recover their properties dragged on for years. As a former Butler associate put it, "I guess you can say Allan Butler has been taken for a ride."

On one level, the story of how the Butlers got victimized is an account of misplaced trust and its consequences. It also shows how Allan Butler may have helped bring on his own undoing by what some observers have considered an unseemly eagerness to convert from small Bahamian banker to big-time financier. And on another level, the story illustrates some of the incredibly convoluted dealings of Vesco, whose talent for financial skullduggery has been seldom matched.

Allan Butler and Vesco present a striking contrast. Butler has the look of a patrician—blond, handsome, introspective. Vesco, with his dark hair, long sideburns and mustache, exudes a street-cocky self-assurance. Butler, son of a well-off Boston physician, is a former captain of the Harvard ski team. Vesco, whose father was a Detroit factory worker, never graduated from college; the forty-year-old promoter (who looks quite a few years younger than his age) got his start peddling aluminum products.

A business deal in the late 1960s brought the two men together. Vesco, then the head of International Controls Corporation, of Fairfield, New Jersey, a maker of electrical and mechanical equipment, retained Butlers Bank to arrange a private sale in Europe of $25 million of debentures for International Controls. Butler was impressed with his client. "Vesco was difficult to deal with," Butler told friends, "but at the eleventh hour he always lived up to his promises." Butler said Vesco was "hardworking, didn't drink and didn't play around with women." At least, such was his estimate of Vesco in 1968.

Butler wasn't alone in his high regard for the New Jersey promoter. He had checked Vesco out with Bank of America, "and he came highly recommended by them." Bank of America, the biggest U.S. bank, thought so much of Vesco that it gave his International Controls company a line of credit of more than $30 million in the late 1960s. And in 1970, the big Prudential Insurance Company of America was only too happy to make a $20 million loan to the Vesco company.

Late in 1970, Vesco turned to Butlers Bank for vital assistance in gaining control of IOS Ltd.

IOS, a Geneva-based, Canadian corporation, collected fees from the sale and management of mutual funds. It also carried on various financial activities, including banking, real estate and the sale of insurance. By late 1969, IOS was facing financial difficulties. The company had grown rapidly, and the payroll had increased faster than could be provided for. A decline in the U.S. stock markets had pushed down the value of the IOS-managed funds, and investors in growing numbers were redeeming their share certificates for cash. Contributing to IOS Ltd's troubles was a series of poor investments by the company, wasteful spending and questionable loans to IOS officials and their business associates.

How Vesco Took a Jet-Set Couple for a Ride

In May 1970, Cornfeld was forced out as chairman of the mutual fund company, and the directors began a frant. search for a savior. Among those who offered to rescue IOS were Europe's Rothschild banking interests and Denver promoter John M. King, who pioneered in the mass merchandising of oil-drilling funds and whose companies eventually collapsed.

None of the talks was successful. Vesco, who had been quietly observing the comings and goings of the business leaders at Bella Vista, the IOS lakeside mansion in Geneva, decided to make his move.

Vesco knew that any attempt to capture control of the vast IOS organization was fraught with risks not only for himself but for International Controls, of which he owned 25 percent, enough to give him a dominant voice in that concern's affairs. In 1967, the Securities and Exchange Commission had imposed a consent decree on Cornfeld's IOS, forbidding the firm from selling shares in its mutual funds in the U.S. or to Americans abroad. The ban stemmed from the refusal of IOS to register with the SEC. Registration would have meant full financial disclosure, an obligation of publicly held companies operating in the U.S. IOS contended that because it was outside the U.S. it was beyond the scrutiny of the SEC. The watchdog agency said in effect: If that's the way you feel about it, you can't do business in the U.S.

Vesco knew that the consent decree stipulated that IOS affiliates also were barred from selling their securities in the U.S. Should the International Controls company gain control of IOS, the SEC might deem it an affiliate of IOS. The implication was clear: As an IOS affiliate, Vesco's International Controls might be proscribed from the sale of its own securities in the U.S. This could be a damaging blow to International Controls, which in the past had raised money through the sale of its shares, traded on the American Stock Exchange.

Yet Vesco pushed ahead. He wanted to get his hands on

25

the large assets that IOS controlled. Despite share redemptions, more than $400 million in securities remained in the four major IOS funds—Fund of Funds, Venture Fund, International Investment Trust and Transglobal Growth Fund. As alleged by the SEC, Vesco seized the reins at IOS, cashed in $224 million of the securities and used a substantial amount of the proceeds for the enrichment of himself and his cronies.

Vesco may well have felt that the SEC would be no match for him in a showdown. After all, almost single-handedly, he had built International Controls' sales from a piddling $1.3 million when he started it in 1965 to more than $100 million by 1969. And he wasn't afraid of a fight. The growth of International Controls had been nourished by its controversial acquisition of Electronic Specialty Company, a West Coast producer of aviation parts and other equipment. The purchase had been angrily opposed by Electronic Specialty's top management, which accused Vesco in a lawsuit of misrepresenting his intentions in seeking to take over the concern. Two federal judges agreed with the charges, but to Vesco's delight, refused to block the acquisition.

Events have made clear that Vesco was counting heavily on his connections in the Republican Party to overcome any SEC opposition to his planned takeover of IOS. In April 1972, some seven months before President Nixon's reelection, Vesco made a secret $200,000 contribution to the Nixon campaign fund.

The payment led to the indictment of Vesco, former Attorney General John Mitchell and former Commerce Secretary Maurice Stans. The charges were that they sought to illegally block the SEC probe into Vesco's growing involvement with IOS in exchange for the large Vesco contribution. A federal grand jury in New York City acquitted Mitchell and Stans in 1974. Vesco, who by then had settled in the tiny central American republic of Costa Rica, wasn't tried on the charges because he had successfully avoided extradition to the U.S.

The Vesco contribution had failed to halt the SEC probe; the SEC's fifty-two-page civil complaint against Vesco, Norman LeBlanc and their colleagues was filed November 27, 1972, just three weeks after Nixon's reelection.

In a typical move, Vesco launched his drive for IOS by disguising his intentions. He only wished to provide ailing IOS with a loan, he had told its directors in the summer of 1970. Naturally, he said, he expected to receive some financial benefits, but he had no desire—none at all—to gain control of the company.

Vesco offered IOS a loan of $5 million to $15 million in the full knowledge that the company had no need to borrow funds. Vesco, who had a sharp eye for the strengths and weaknesses of a company, had quickly realized that IOS's financial problems weren't nearly as serious as the board of directors had been led to believe. Liquidity could easily be achieved by the sale of IOS's Italian operation, a mutual fund management and sales company, which the Italian government was pressuring IOS to sell anyway.

Vesco persuaded the IOS board that the company badly needed a loan even though its cash position was basically sound. The naivete of the directors was nicely described by New Jersey Judge Melvin Antell in a May 1975 ruling against Vesco in connection with a suit brought by IOS stockholders. "IOS's management" said the judge, "while highly successful in creating an aggressive and productive sales organization, was largely unschooled in the dynamics of corporate finance." Vesco put it another way: "They were too dumb to know that they didn't need the money."

Vesco offered to make available to IOS a substantial part of the $20 million that International Controls had previously borrowed from Prudential Insurance Company of America. However, Vesco neglected to inform IOS that the loan agreement with Prudential excluded the use of the

27

money for such purposes as those that Vesco had now proposed. This presented a problem for Vesco because IOS had told him that before it could accept a loan from him it had to get confirmation from banks that International Controls had possession of the cash. This meant that IOS needed bank assurance that the $20 million from Prudential was in International Control's name; but at the same time, if Vesco was to succeed, no mention could be made by the bank of any restrictions upon the use of the money.

The persuasive Vesco secured the cooperation of Wilbert J. Snipes, senior vice president of American National Bank and Trust Company, Morristown, New Jersey, who sent the requested telex from his institution, and that of various officials of Butlers Bank Ltd., who also accommodated Vesco's request that IOS not be told the money couldn't be made available, according to Judge Antell. Mr. Snipes was a board member of International Controls, the judge added, while the "active connivance" of Butlers Bank was obtained by the promise that the bank would receive large deposits.

The upshot was that Vesco arranged for International Controls to make a $5 million loan to IOS Ltd. The appreciative directors awarded Vesco with three seats on the IOS board and made Vesco chairman of the all-important IOS finance committee, which had the power to pass on all expenses over $1,000. In addition, International Controls was granted warrants to buy four million IOS shares.

In arranging the $5 million for IOS, Vesco got International Controls to put up only $1 million. The other $4 million was subsequently borrowed by International Controls from Butlers Bank. This represented a considerable undertaking for the Bahamian bank. It had a net worth of only $5 million. In making a $4 million loan, it could have found itself strapped for cash in the event of heavy depositors' withdrawals. All this was explained to Vesco, who arranged for $4 million to be put in Butlers Bank as a compensating deposit for the $4 million loan.

Where did Butlers Bank obtain the $4 million deposit? It came, of all places, from IOS, which had sold its Italian operation for $10 million and deposited $4 million in Butlers Bank. Vesco had induced IOS to deposit the money in Butlers Bank by telling the IOS directors that this would clear the way for big loans to IOS from two major U.S. banks.

Consider what Vesco had accomplished. He had got his foot inside IOS's door by duping the company into believing it needed an infusion of $5 million in cash. He then got IOS to put $4 million of its own money into Butlers Bank, freeing the bank to lend that same $4 million to International Controls, so that International Controls in turn could lend the $4 million (plus $1 million of its own money) back to IOS Ltd.

IOS, without realizing it, was being "rescued" with its own money. Such hocus-pocus by Vesco might be regarded as high comedy if the end result hadn't been the collapse of IOS. (Incidentally, International Controls repaid this $4 million loan to Butlers Bank).

A few months later, Vesco sealed his grip on IOS by purchasing Bernard Cornfeld's control block of six million shares with a $5.5 million loan supplied by the ever-helpful Butlers Bank. This time, Vesco induced the Arthur Lipper Corporation, a New York stock brokerage firm that depended on brokerage transactions with the IOS funds for a substantial amount of its income, to make a $5.5 million deposit in Butlers Bank. The bank was supposed to get the Cornfeld shares as collateral for the loan, but it never got them. "Vesco wouldn't give the shares up," a source close to Butler says. "He kept them in a safe deposit box in Switzerland."

To conceal his purchase of the IOS shares from the SEC, Vesco arranged for a newly created company, Linkink Progressive Corporation, of Panama, to buy Cornfeld's six million shares. Cornfeld, documents show, was bitterly opposed to Vesco, and Cornfeld mistakenly believed he was selling his stock to certain large banks that were represented as being eager to gain a voice in IOS's affairs. But Linkink then sold the shares to Red Pearl Bay, another supposedly independent Panama company, which in turn sold for a nominal amount the six million IOS shares to American Interland, a newly formed Canadian subsidiary of Vesco-led International Controls.

The failure of Butlers Bank to obtain the IOS shares as collateral would not have posed a big problem had the $5.5 million loan been repaid in full. But as it turned out, nearly $4 million of the $5.5 million never made its way back to Butlers Bank, leaving the bank with a serious liquidity problem.

Why did Butler involve his bank in these maneuvers? "You have to understand Allan's attitude at the time," a Butler friend explained. "IOS under Cornfeld was in financial trouble. Allan felt an IOS collapse could bring down a lot of financial institutions. He felt anything he could do to get IOS away from Cornfeld he should."

But Butler's motives weren't entirely altruistic. Vesco had promised that the IOS funds and their affiliates would pump large deposits into Butlers Bank in return for the vital assistance the bank had given Vesco.

Moreover, Vesco led Butler to believe that the Butlers would be given control of a big new holding company that would embrace banks owned by IOS as well as Butlers Bank. "Allan had wanted to build up Butlers Bank into an international bank, and along comes Vesco and promises the moon," a Butler friend said.

An acquaintance of Butler said that the banker was also motivated by a desire to emerge from the shadow of his wife, Shirley. "Allan is always being described as 'Shirley's husband,'" related the acquaintance. "I used to kid him, 'You're a member of Husbands Anonymous.' I think Allan wanted to show what he could do on his own, and he felt Vesco could help him."

Meanwhile, Butlers Bank was in serious financial straits. It had made bad investments and needed additional cash. Its problems stemmed from the use of short-term deposits to make long-term loans. When some of them went sour, the bank had insufficient funds to repay depositors.

By October 1971, Butlers Bank was so short of cash that it sold some $7.3 million of assets to Bahamas Commonwealth Bank, a newly formed Nassau bank which Vesco controlled. The sale gave Butlers Bank an estimated $1.5 million profit.

A former U.S. government investigator said that Vesco, in aiding Butlers Bank, had acted out of self-interest. The source explained that the Bahamian government of Premier Lynden Pindling had agreed to allow Vesco to operate Bahamas Commonwealth provided that Butlers Bank was kept afloat. According to the source, "Pindling was afraid that if Butlers Bank collapsed it would scare off foreign investors. There were too many banks collapsing in the Bahamas."

Bahamas Commonwealth, which the government shut down later, in June 1974, on the ground it operated in a manner detrimental to depositors and other creditors, played a central role in Vesco's alleged looting of the IOS funds. The bank was used as a conduit for the diversion of cash from the IOS funds into a variety of Vesco-controlled companies that he formed in the Western Hemisphere.

Aggravating the problems of Butlers Bank was a shortage of able executives. "Allan was running the whole show, and he had no backup management," says a Butler acquaintance. "Some of the management had left because they didn't like Butler's dealing with Vesco. Also, Allan is quiet and very secretive, and some found him difficult to work for."

By the summer of 1972, the financial condition of Butlers Bank had greatly deteriorated. The Butlers reluctantly decided they must sell Lewis-Oakes Ltd., which controlled Butlers Bank, Security Capital Corporation, General

Bahamian Companies, and Charlotte Street Properties, owner of the Nassau office building and parking lot.

The Butlers' reasons for this decision were varied. The disintegration of the bank was one. There were also rumors that the Pindling regime was looking upon their operations with disfavor; certain black executives at Butler companies in Nassau were active in the Free National Movement, a minority political group opposed to Mr. Pindling. "The Butlers were hearing rumors that they were suspected of financing the Pindling opposition, which was completely untrue and terribly upsetting to them," a Butler friend said. "Vesco kept the Butlers on edge by telling them that they were persona non grata in the Bahamas."

Several incidents gave credence to the rumors. A foreign bookkeeper, whom a Butler company in Nassau was extremely eager to hire, wasn't able to obtain a work permit from the government. Another Butler company, for reasons that the government never explained, was forced to wait unduly before it received a renewal of its license to do business.

Butler suffered another setback when efforts by Security Capital Corporation, which he controlled, to pull off a major acquisition in Canada fell through—at considerable expense to Security Capital. Butler had long nourished the hope of shifting the base of his operations from Nassau to Canada. His plan had called for Security Capital to acquire Seaway Multi-Corporation, a widely diversified Toronto concern. Following that acquisition, the Butlers had intended to put Butlers Bank and other Bahamian assets under the corporate umbrella of Security Capital.

It came as a shock to Allan Butler when certain English and Canadian banks, with whom his bank had enjoyed long-time relationships, refused to lend the money to enable Security Capital to buy control of Seaway Multi-Corporation. "The reason for their action was quite plain," a Butler acquaintance explained. "It was because of Butler's association with Vesco. Vesco was bad medicine."

The acquaintance added: "I think Butler then realized for the first time he never should've gotten mixed up with Vesco."

Allan Butler's desire to shift ownership of his Bahamian assets to a Canadian company was an outgrowth of the apparent antibusiness attitude of the Pindling regime. In the late 1960s, Butler had planned to sell shares of Butlers Bank to the public. The plan was shelved after the Pindling regime, which took power in 1967, made it increasingly difficult for white expatriates in the Bahamas to obtain renewals of their work permits. The regime's explanation: Black Bahamians, who composed more than 85 percent of the population, would forever remain waiters and street vendors unless pressure was put on white-owned businesses in the Bahamas to train blacks for office jobs held by white employees.

The effect of the government's policy was to discourage foreign investment in the Bahamas. As a result, Butler dropped his plans to sell shares of Butlers Bank to the public. According to a Butler acquaintance, "It would have been impossible to attract investor interest because of the uncertainties with the black government. That's why Allan wanted to build up his Canadian base and put the Bahamian parts in it. The feeling was that Pindling wouldn't want to mess around with any of the Bahamian assets if they were part of a Canadian company."

The failure of Security Capital to acquire Seaway Multi-Corporation was the final blow. "It got to be too much for Allan, and he came down with pneumonia," a Butler friend said. "He was completely drained. He was trying to run Butlers Bank, as well as General Bahamian Companies. He'd been going all out on that Security Capital deal. He was also testifying at the SEC investigation of Vesco. He had to be three hundred places at once, and it got to be too much."

So in 1972, Butler turned to Robert Vesco. "Allan felt he needed some kind of help to save his companies," a Butler friend said. "He felt a keen obligation to protect all his employees under the Lewis-Oakes banner, as well as shareholders, and the depositors of Butlers Bank. Physically as well as psychologically, it was a painful time for him. His wife's money had helped to found the companies—essentially the $3 million with which to start Butler's Bank. He felt he had to pull the companies through, not only for the others, but to reassure himself of his own abilities. With all his troubles, he'd begun to have doubts as to his abilities. The trouble was, there were few people other than Vesco that he could turn to for help."

Allan Butler went to bed one night hardly able to breathe. His lungs were congested from pneumonia. It was then he decided he must make a move. "He offered Vesco a management contract to take over Butlers Bank and the other businesses," his friend and associate said.

Vesco was flattered that the Butlers held him in such high regard, but he rejected the offer. Instead, he proposed that he, Vesco, buy Lewis-Oakes Ltd., thereby removing at one stroke all of the Butlers' worries over their various companies. How much did the Butlers want for their assets? "There was no way to do a quick estimate of all the sixty-odd companies that made up the Lewis-Oakes holdings. So we said, 'Give Shirley Butler back her $3 million that she originally invested, and you have a deal,'" the Butler friend said. "Vesco's eyes lit up. At the time, the assets of Lewis-Oakes looked to be worth far in excess of $3 million. The deal was made."

But Vesco refused Butler's demands that Vesco personally buy Lewis-Oakes. Instead, Vesco said that a newly formed company would serve as purchaser. "That didn't make me happy," said the Butler associate. "I preferred Vesco's personal obligation rather than the obligation of a shell company. With a shell, you don't get much." Facing a take it or leave it ultimatum, the Butlers accepted Vesco's condition. "We then asked for his personal guarantee on the notes. Vesco said no. We asked for collateral. He said no. It was no, no, no," said the Butler associate.

After agreement was reached, Vesco called in Norman LeBlanc and dictated the "structure of the agreed transaction," according to an affidavit by Shirley Butler. LeBlanc, a 39-year-old former Toronto accountant, had impressed Vesco with his financial acumen, and Vesco had made him chief financial officer at IOS.

Fairborn Corporation Ltd., a Bahamian company that LeBlanc headed, purchased on August 17 1972, all of Lewis-Oakes' 2,876,777 outstanding shares for $3 million in promissory notes. Fairborn, which had no assets except five issued shares each worth one dollar, said it would pay the notes off over a three-year period.

One year later, in August 1973, LeBlanc said Fairborn couldn't make payment on the first note, then due, and asked for an extension. Shirley Butler said that was impossible. The forceful Mrs. Butler then threatened Fairborn and LeBlanc with a judgement. The upshot: Fairborn made a $300,000 payment and a promise to pay the $700,000 balance on the first note within six months.

It's worth noting that LeBlanc's $300,000 payment to the Butlers may have been drawn indirectly from one of the IOS mutual funds. The payment was made by Global Financial Ltd., one of the myriad of Vesco-LeBlanc shell companies. Global Financial, according to the SEC, had earlier obtained $10 million in cash from Venture Fund, one of the IOS funds that Vesco allegedly looted. Thus, investors in Venture Fund, without realizing it, may have helped the Vesco group to acquire Shirley Butler's Lewis-Oakes Ltd.

When it came time for Fairborn to pay the $700,000 in February 1973, LeBlanc told Shirley Butler, "I won't pay," and disclosed that Fairborn was insolvent and was to be liquidated.

The honeymoon with the Vesco group was over.

Swindled!

Disillusionment actually may have set in sooner. Said a Butler associate: "When the Butlers made the deal to sell Lewis-Oakes in August 1972, I didn't think Vesco was a crook. But then came the SEC complaint of November 1972. That complaint spelled it all out. It was an eye opener. I knew then that we were in the soup."

To collect the remaining $2.7 million owed by Fairborn, Shirley Butler sued the company, Vesco and LeBlanc. The Butlers realized they might have a tough time collecting. They asked the Bahamas court to seize the assets that Mrs. Butler had sold to LeBlanc's Fairborn Corporation Ltd. Haste was imperative, lest LeBlanc throw a legal roadblock in their path by transferring control of Fairborn from himself to some other person or property.

The Butlers didn't move quickly enough.

Mrs. Butler, her husband and their attorney met with Vesco and LeBlanc at Vesco's home on Brace Ridge Road in Nassau on February 19 1974 to discuss the $2.7 million owed to Mrs. Butler. "At that meeting," according to Mrs. Butler's affidavit, "I asked Mr. LeBlanc who held the shares of Fairborn Corporation, and he replied to the effect that he was not sure, but that directly or indirectly he owned the same personally."

The Butlers' attorney asked LeBlanc to be more specific. Were the shares, asked the attorney, held in a trust? Or how were they held? LeBlanc replied, "I don't know where they are, but I think they might be in 'Antler'." Asked what "Antler" might be, LeBlanc is said to have answered, "It is just a Bahamian holding company. I have some forty shell companies that I keep putting on top of one another to keep people from finding out what's going on. Of course they are only good for so long, then I put another on top."

Mrs. Butler wasn't amused. "Mr. LeBlanc's statement revealed a calculated and cynical pattern of dealing designed to remove valuable assets out of reach of creditors

and shareholders for the purpose of benefitting Mr. Le-
Blanc and his associates," she said in her affidavit.

(Vesco is alleged by the SEC to have scattered much of
the $224 million he took out of the IOS funds over various
jurisdictions through tiers of companies he controlled. For
example, Vesco had Fund of Funds, one of the IOS funds,
invest $60 million in a Costa Rican company that the Vesco
group formed. The money was then transferred to a
newly-formed Panamanian company, which transferred
the money to a Vesco-controlled Bahamian bank. "It was
nothing more than a shell game to prevent any future tracing," says the SEC.)

LeBlanc, like Vesco, is now in Costa Rica. He and Vesco
have claimed they did nothing wrong so far as the Butlers
are concerned, and that they aren't liable for any debts
incurred by Fairborn Corporation. LeBlanc has insisted he
was merely Fairborn's agent.

If the Butlers were confused by the goings-on, Robert
Slatter, a Nassau accountant, was confused, too. He was
hired by the Bahamas court as Fairborn's liquidator to track
down the missing assets Fairborn had purchased from
Shirley Butler. Slatter quickly learned that the job of
liquidator might even tax the talents of Sherlock Holmes.

As an example, consider the journey of the control block
of Security Capital shares, part of the property Fairborn
obtained from the Butlers. LeBlanc first stored most of
those shares in two Fairborn subsidiaries named W. B.
Holdings Ltd. and W.H.O. Holdings Ltd. In February
1974, at the time that Mrs. Butler filed suit, the Security
Capital shares were transferred by LeBlanc from the two
subsidiaries to an entity called Moropan Holdings Inc. The
head of Moropan Holdings, which was based in Panama,
was Eusebio Morales, a director of Vesco's Bahamas
Commonwealth Bank.

According to Slatter, the liquidator of Fairborn, Moropan
Holdings paid for the shares of Security Capital with a note

of Moropan Holdings, "which does not appear to have any other assets." Slatter described the transfer of the shares to Moropan as fraudulent and urged cancellation of the sale by the Bahamas court. By May 1975, the matter was still unresolved, and as a lawyer puts it, "This whole thing could take ten years to straighten out."

What the lawyer feared was that Moropan Holdings might insist that it bought in good faith the Security Capital shares from Fairborn and intended to keep them. Or, the lawyer speculated, the court might rule in the Butlers' favor and order Moropan Holdings to return the shares to Slatter, Fairborn's liquidator: by then, however, Moropan Holdings might have already "sold" the shares to a newly-formed shell based, for example, in San Salvador. The Butlers would then face the task of collecting evidence to show that the transfer of Security Capital's shares to the San Salvador firm was a fraudulent scheme concocted by Vesco-LeBlanc, which might take several more years.

The question of who rightfully owned the Security Capital shares was, naturally enought, critical to the management of Security Capital. The block of shares in question represented over 40 percent of the company's voting stock. The matter was also of interest to the Ontario Securities Commission, which in July 1973 had halted trading of Security Capital shares on the Toronto Stock Exchange pending clarification of the ownership.

Norman LeBlanc, of all people, helped to shed a little light on the controversy. In June 1974, he sent a cable to Security Capital's management declaring that he controlled Moropan Holdings, which he said, owned a controlling block of Security Capital shares. LeBlanc then demanded that W. Edward Barnes, Security Capital's president, call a meeting of stockholders so that LeBlanc could vote his more than 40 percent interest to oust Security Capital's directors, including Barnes. In other words, Barnes should institute an action to have himself fired. LeBlanc's anger at Barnes was apparently triggered by LeBlanc's removal as a director of General Bahamian Companies, which Security Capital controlled.

, LeBlanc was told by Security Capital's management that it would refuse to call a stockholders meeting and that it didn't recognize Moropan Holdings of Panama as rightful owner of the Security Capital shares. Since then, liquidator Slatter has taken the position that most of the Security Capital shares in question were still registered in the name of W. B. Holdings, the subsidiary of Fairborn. The Butlers welcomed this news, of course, because liquidator Slatter was in charge of W. B. Holdings.

There was also the question of the whereabouts of the shares of Charlotte Street Properties, owner of the Nassau office building and parking lot. These shares were among the assets sold to Fairborn by Mrs. Butler's Lewis-Oakes Ltd. It is known that the shares were originally assigned by LeBlanc to W.H.O. Holdings, another Fairborn subsidiary.

To quote from an affidavit Slatter gave to the Bahamas court: "When I requested the shares and other records of Charlotte Street Properties, I was informed that Charlotte Street Properties had been sold by W.H.O. Holdings and was, therefore, no longer an asset of (Fairborn Corporation) or its subsidiary (W.H.O. Holdings). The sale of Charlotte Street Properties by W.H.O. Holdings was not known to W.H.O.'s secretary, and was not recorded in W.H.O.'s minute books or accounting records. I was then advised," Slatter goes on, "that the sale had been by an 'agreement,' but a copy was not available as the only executed copy was in the personal file of Mr. Norman LeBlanc." It wasn't necessary for liquidator Slatter to add that the secretive LeBlanc wasn't going to turn over that copy.

Slatter, a man of dogged perseverance, still managed to track down the Charlotte Street Properties shares. They had been transferred to Property Resources Ltd., a subsidiary of Value Capital Ltd. Value Capital, it turns out, according to the SEC complaint against Vesco, was a holding company formed by the Vesco group to serve as a receptacle for some of the assets that Vesco allegedly looted from IOS.

If it was any comfort to the Butlers, Norman LeBlanc lost one of the greatly cherished assets that he had obtained from Allan Butler. This was a Sabreliner jet, which Le-Blanc's Fairborn Corporation, in a separate transaction, acquired from Butler back in 1972.

As payment for the jet, Butler has asserted in yet another suit against LeBlanc, LeBlanc promised to put $10 million of assets into Fairborn. These assets were to serve as collateral for the $3 million in promissory notes that Shirley Butler got when she sold Lewis-Oakes Ltd. to the Fairborn company. But LeBlanc failed to deposit the $10 million of assets in Fairborn, according to a court document. Instead, he arranged for Fairborn to sell the Sabreliner for one dollar and "other consideration" to none other than himself. In turn, LeBlanc, having "purchased" the jet from Fairborn, a company he owned, turned around and "sold" it for a purported $10,000 to Property Resources, a subsidiary of Value Capital, which Vesco-LeBlanc had created.

The Butlers once more went to court and obtained an order forbidding the removal of the Sabreliner from the Nassau airport. In defiance of the order, an unknown person boarded it and flew to Costa Rica. It seemed as if one more asset had gotten away. However, an unidentified pilot again secretly boarded the jet at Costa Rica's San Jose airport and flew it to the U.S. LeBlanc was outraged. He publicly charged that the jet's disappearance was one more example of the harassment to which he says he has been subjected to because of his close ties to Robert Vesco. His outcry fell on unsympathetic ears.

Mrs. Butler's Lewis-Oakes Ltd. is in a shambles. Butlers Bank is in liquidation. But the Butlers still manage to live in comfort. "Their living standards are higher than yours and mine," a Butler acquaintance said. They still have the Jacaranda house in Nassau, an apartment on Manhattan's elegant East Side and land on Martha's Vineyard.

Not long ago, a Bahamian court returned to Shirley Butler control of Security Capital, though the concern will require a new infusion of capital from the Butlers. Allan Butler, meanwhile, had settled his differences with the SEC, leaving him, perhaps in a wiser way, to engage in new ventures.

III

Equity Funding:
"I Did It For The Jollies"
By William E. Blundell

If Beacon Street in Boston has the aroma of Old Money and Wall Street is redolent of Big Money, then there hangs over the Avenue of the Stars the crisp, raw smell of New Money. This singular boulevard bisects a commercial, residential, business and entertainment complex in Los Angeles known as Century City. Designed as a self-contained urban tomorrowland, it is as pretty and patterned as the architects' drawings; amid the song of fountains and the flutter of flags, office towers rise sleekly from lawns banked with flowers. It all looks rather too good to be true. The same could have been said of its most notorious tenant, Equity Funding Corporation of America.

Equity Funding was an "idea company." In the soaring sixties, when it went public and became a hot stock, an idea was all you really needed. Carloads of hungry money poured into anything with certain buzz words in the corporate title: computer, systems, micro-this or that. Sometimes it didn't matter what the company actually *did*. The grandly titled Performance Systems Inc. peddled fried chicken, and not very good fried chicken at that.

Century City was and is a lodestone for idea companies, the hot young lawyers who serve them, the consultants, the guys with a gimmick. Far down Wilshire Boulevard in the old downtown area, the big conservative banks, oil com-

42

panies and other long-entrenched businesses soberly managed their assets to minimize the chance of loss. But out on the West Side, in Century City and adjacent Beverly Hills, the swingers clustered.

They managed assets to maximize the chance for profit. If that often did not materialize, if, distressingly, a shortsighted world was not ready for solar toilets or hamster tax-shelters or a particular synergistic miniconglomerate—well, it was not their own money the idea men were playing with. Tough luck, suckers.

There has never been a shortage of the latter among the residents of the West Side, which may house more *nouveaux riches* per acre than any place outside the Middle East. These self-made men, their fortunes just beginning to bloom, their backgrounds in finance sketchy, are eager to listen to those who have new ideas on how to make their money grow fast. In such a deep pool of capital thick with such fat fish, sharks are inevitable. So the West Side has had more than its share of business scandals and failures in recent years, with investors disconsolately picking their way through the ruins of bombed-out tax shelters, unstrung conglomerates, collapsed brokerages and commodity options schemes blown to bits.

But the biggest explosion was that of Equity Funding. The company fit its surroundings perfectly: it was big, new, aggressive, obsessed with rapid growth, and it pushed an idea that gave it powerful investor appeal. This was the so-called Equity Funding concept. In its execution, a purchaser first bought from an Equity Funding salesman a life-insurance policy and some mutual-fund shares.

He paid for the shares, but then left them with the company, which used them as collateral for a loan it gave him to pay his policy premium. This procedure was followed for ten years, the company expanding its loan year by year to pay the annual policy premium, the insured buying, year by year, enough additional fund shares to keep his expanding loan collateralized. At the end of ten years the program was to end. The insured would pay off his loan and interest (usually with some of his fund shares). He would keep the rest of his shares and an insurance policy with cash value. He would have beaten the game, gotten something for nothing.

That assumes, of course, that the mutual fund shares were growing in value. Little was said about what would happen in a prolonged market slump, which would leave the insured with a capital loss on his shares, the loan to repay, and the interest. But in those bullish times no one appreciated that eventuality.

At first, Equity Funding was just an agency, selling policies and mutual funds underwritten and sponsored by other firms. But you didn't get to be a hot stock by just tending to your knitting, and beginning in 1967, three years after going public, the company started swallowing up all manner of other concerns in the carnivorous fashion of the day—winding up, by mid-1972, the owner of three insurance companies of its own, mutual-fund management and sales operations, savings-and-loans associations, real-estate companies, oil and gas concessions, a cattle-breeding outfit, and a Bahamian bank.

Wow, said Wall Street. Along the way Equity Funding became the fastest-growing financial-services concern on Fortune's list. The year it went public it earned a measly $390,000 on revenues of $2.9 million; when the roof caved in it was ready to report earnings for 1972 of $22.6 million on revenues of $152.6 million. It listed assets approaching $750 million and a net worth of $143.4 million.

Or so the company said. The whole thing was a mirage, and in a few short weeks in the spring of 1973 Equity funding, as everyone had known it, simply disappeared. Subsequent investigation disclosed that since it had gone public it had *never* made any money. Its earnings all those years were fake, Its assets were bloated and its liabilities hidden. The money it had raised from bank loans and debenture offerings had been soaked up in covering its real losses. It had created out of thin air $2 billion worth of insurance that its agents had never written—and then resold it for cash to trusting reinsurers. It had gulled some of its auditors and suborned others, who then conspired with it in a swindle that lasted almost a decade. "Why did you do it, for God's sake, why?" an anguished banker asked one of the executive ringleaders. He looked at the banker and said, "I did it for the jollies."

That was not an entirely facetious answer. The methodology of the fraud at Equity Funding and its tremendous impact on various institutions has been dissected by financial writers. But there has been baffled silence on a central question—what possessed men, some of them professionals in specialties with clearly defined codes of ethics, men whose prior brushes with the law had amounted to traffic violations, to do what they did?

Twenty employees and two outside auditors of the company were indicted on federal charges in the case, including the chairman and president, several executive vice presidents, and a clutch of vice presidents and other managers. In the course of the fraud, these ordinary suburbanites, these guys next door, had engaged in lying, forgery, counterfeiting, bugging, embezzlement, and multiple forms of fraud that had victimized thousands of unwary people, costing them hundreds of millions of dollars.

But the criminals were victims too, sucked into a vortex they did not have the strength or the will to escape. Gradually, the conspiracy of which they were a part seemed to take on a life of its own, and grew so enormous, so voracious, that it made vassals even of the men who had designed it and thought they were its masters. They could not halt it. By then, some had been so transformed by it that they did not care; they had grown to enjoy their bondage, and thus knew true evil. They were, in an awful sense, doing it for the jollies.

It is easy to label their motives. Money? Certainly with

some it was very important. But it is also true that many of the conspirators got absolutely nothing out of the scheme, and didn't ask to; they cheerfully slaved eighty hours a week to enrich their superiors and in the end went down clutching worthless company stock. Corporate loyalty? Some of that, yes—but for others it was a joke. One defendant hated corporate life and the values it represented to him. Others felt they owed nothing at all to Equity Funding as a corporation.

So labels say little. But there is a lesson. Corporations can and do create a moral tone that powerfully influences the thinking, conduct, values and even the personalities of the people who work for them. This tone is set by the men who run the company, and their corruption can quickly corrupt all else. A startling thing about Equity Funding is how rarely one finds, in a cast of characters big enough to make a war movie, a man who said, "No, I won't do that. It's wrong." As for the majority who were sucked in and drowned, their motives were many and mixed. The important thing is that the fraud unerringly pressed upon their weaknesses, some of which they were unaware of at the time, and quickly overthrew them almost before they realized what had happened.

It all began, as Equity Funding itself began, with the enigmatic but menacing figure of Stanley Goldblum, a founder and chief executive of the company until the fraud was uncovered. Goldblum was one of five men who started Equity Funding in 1960. There was bickering, there were buyouts, and soon only two were left, Goldblum and Michael Riordan. Both had been salesmen, Goldblum in life insurance and Riordan a wholesaler in mutual funds, but there all similarity ended.

Riordan went to Cornell, came from money and moved through life on wheels greased by it and by his own huge Irish expansiveness. He cut across all class lines. If Wall

Equity Funding: "I Did It for the Jollies"

Street investment bankers and lawyers were his friends, so were denizens of the Manhattan bars where he drank the nights away. He loved parties, 100-mph spins in his Lincoln, a turn of the cards. Riordan's magnetism rose naturally from sheer warmth and unbounded enthusiasm. He wanted to smell the flowers while he could, and there was hardly a bouquet that went untested when he was on the scene.

Goldblum was his polar opposite. His father was a jeweler of small means, and Goldblum's dream of becoming a physician was stifled. Dropping out of UCLA short of his degree, he got a job hauling scrap. Later he would join his father-in-law in the meat-packing business, shoving tons of beef around every day, making sausage, just to earn a buck. It wasn't until 1955, when he was twenty-eight, that he turned to life insurance, eventually joining the partnership that evolved into Equity Funding.

He became a millionaire before he was forty, but money did not warm him. By all accounts, he was extraordinarily quick and shrewd, but aloof, hard and curt with subordinates. His private life remained private. He was no bon vivant. While Riordan partied, Goldblum sweated in his $100,000 gym, behind his house, a silent man, pumping iron, maintaining an awesome physique; at six feet, two inches, 235 pounds of bone and muscle, he was physically intimidating. His eyes were chilly, and high cheekbones gave his face an Oriental cast. He had a cold, commanding manner that oozed power. Always seizing an initiative, giving the orders, dominating every meeting, he was as much emperor as chief executive.

It was not easy to talk to such a man, especially if you were several rungs below him on the corporate ladder. Goldblum knew it. He had a dark sense of humor, sometimes exercised at his own expense. He once characterized himself as "an imposing figure, a threatening authority figure. I'm not a gregarious fellow."

Most people mired in the fraud couldn't bring them-

47

selves to complain to Goldblum. Says one conspirator, a lowly vice president: "I never went up top. You looked at Goldblum and you knew you'd never get anywhere with him. He was such a grim man; I never saw him smile but once. That was when we were bugging the offices that the regulators were using for the audit of the company's books. Goldblum said, 'If they catch you, tell them the bad guys over there (waving to the offices of some executive vice presidents) told you to do it.'"

Gary Beckerman, a young manager involved in a counterfeiting scheme, asked for a vacation. "You're going to stay," said Goldblum flatly. "I don't know why I didn't up and leave anyway," Beckerman recalls. "If it had been anyone else I would have said, 'kiss my ass!' But Goldblum had this tremendous presence . . ."

For all their differences, Goldblum and Riordan were close. The latter was almost certainly an architect of the early stages of the fraud, but his precise responsibility will probably never be fixed; he died in an uniquely Los Angeles fashion in 1969 when a mudslide triggered by heavy rains rolled down a hillside and through the wall of his canyon home, smothering him. Stanley Goldblum took the Riordan family into his house. "He was the greatest guy I ever met," said Goldblum, and years afterward, when his ornate office was seized upon disclosure of the fraud, only one personal thing would be found in it—a photograph of Mike Riordan.

If Riordan helped design the fraud, Goldblum played the major part in nourishing it into the devouring thing it eventually became. Riordan, as chairman, dealt with the sales force and with banks and Wall Street. Goldblum, the president, ran the internal affairs of the company—"the bookkeeper in the background," as he has been called. In late 1964, just after Equity Funding went public, the bookkeeper took what was probably the first step into the morass.

He told Jerome Evans, then Equity Funding's treasurer, to post as income money that the company hadn't yet received—commissions, he told Evans, that were due the company from brokerage firms involved in transactions with Equity Funding. Because it would have been improper to list these 'give up' commissions as such, Evans was told that he should post them in the books as ordinary commissions received on the sales of mutual fund-life insurance packages.

There weren't any commissions. This was the beginning of what has been called the 'funding fraud.' The funding concept, under which a buyer of the mutual fund-insurance package was granted loans on his shares to pay his policy premiums, yielded income to the company in several ways. The company got commissions on the sale of the funds and the insurance, and interest on the loan. It then paid out part of this income in commissions to the individual agents who did the actual selling, and in interest on the money it had to borrow itself to extend the policyholder loans. What was left was profit. Now what if the company claimed phony commission income? First, its revenues would look larger than they really were. Second, net income, or profit, could be similarly inflated at an even greater rate, since there were no real agents' commissions and other expenses to pay. Third, phony assets could be added to the books in the form of "loans receivable" from phony borrowers.

All the scheme required were complaisant outside auditors, which Equity Funding had in men from Wolfson, Weiner and Company; the sabotage of the internal auditing function, easily accomplished by simple neglect, and the knowledge of the few people who actually made false entries and ordered them. Only those who needed to know needed to be told. With hardly more than a few pencil strokes, the company could be made to look bigger, more efficient and more financially stable than it was.

Evans posted phony figures in the books at the end of 1964 and waited for the cash to come in. It didn't. Evans asked about it, and Goldblum assured him it was coming; meanwhile, there were even more "give up" commissions for Evans to put on the books for the first quarter. Reluctantly, Evans did so. Strand after fine strand, for quarter after quarter, the web was cast over Evans until, in time, he found he could not resist at all. By now he knew there were no real commissions coming; Goldblum knew he knew, and the pretense was dropped. Year after year, Evans doctored the books at Goldblum's order. The president no longer even bothered to give Evans a commission figure— just an earnings-per-share target that Evans was to meet. The arithmetic was up to Evans.

The steady upward march of the company's reported earnings, revenues and assets impressed Wall Street. Equity Funding's stock soared.

That was the purpose of the fraud. Goldblum had founder's shares in the company, as did Riordan, and both got rich. Goldblum was to make $5 million in stock; Riordan and his estate, $19 million. Beyond that, a high stock price was necessary to motivate Equity Funding's army of salesmen, lured to the company in part by a generous stock incentive program. And the bloated stock and asset figures were the keystone in Equity Funding's success in acquiring other companies in exchange for stock, in floating bond offerings and in otherwise borrowing money.

The treatment of Evans by Goldblum; the encouragement to do what seemed at first a little thing, for a plausible reason; then the request to do it again and yet again, until finally there was no excuse, just an assumption that the subordinate was now firmly enmeshed in the conspiracy, run through the Equity Funding tale. "Nothing was ever laid out completely to me," says Larry Collins, a former officer jailed for his part. "It all evolved in little bits and pieces, gradually; it took a long time before it finally hit you that you were committing a crime. 'Don't worry,' they said. That's what they *always* said at Equity Funding. 'Don't worry.' "

Equity Funding: "I Did It for the Jollies"

Evans kept plugging in phony figures and, year by year, sweated out the annual audits; certainly the auditors were complaisant, but still they needed certain assurances, even if these were lies, to justify the skewed figures they were reviewing. Early in 1969, just after Riordan died, and shortly after Evans himself had a heart attack, Evans could face it no longer. One day he left the office, packed his bags and drove aimlessly around the country for six weeks. He never returned to the company.

By now, after five years of falsification, Equity Funding's books were horribly distorted; assets in "funded loans receivable" were so bloated that it was nearly impossible to cover up the enormous discrepancy between the phony figure and the real. The audit of 1968 results was beginning, and the conspirators had lost Riordan and Evans.

The difficulties at Equity Funding were compounded by the arrival there of a couple of honest men. One was Harry Watkins, inexplicably assigned by the auditors to coordinate the 1968 audit. The other was a financial man, John Templeton, hired as controller by Equity Funding in late 1968 and later asked to take over Evans' audit chores after Evans disappeared.

Templeton just couldn't find any real evidence that Equity Funding had the $36 million in funded loans receivable that the books said it had. Then Harry Watkins did something that other members of his firm evidently had never bothered to do before. He pressed for the evidence, demanding a list of all those policyholders with funded loans outstanding so he could verify that they really had borrowed and owed the money. A computer run totaled their debts; the money due Equity Funding amounted to just $7.6 million.

This touched off a desperate scramble by the conspirators to somehow explain nearly $30 million in ephemeral assets. Goldblum gave Templeton the old story about the receipt of brokerage-house commissions concealed as ordinary commissions on funded programs and posted as loans receivable on the books. Fine, said Templeton; explain that to the auditor. No, said Goldblum.

At Goldblum's direction, Templeton then started on a course of justification, adding terminated loans, new business and other dubious entries to try to cover the discrepancy. At this point, he too was in danger of being sucked in. The troublesome Watkins was whisked off the audit entirely, and a more reasonable bean counter substituted. Templeton stood alone and under great pressure.

However, none of the coverups completely succeeded, and Goldblum himself finally had to trot out the tall tale about commissions for the auditors. He added that Riordan, who had just died, had been the only man who kept track of these commissions, and the total was now lost. The auditors bought this remarkable story and the "evidence" that Templeton reluctantly compiled to verify the claimed $36 million in loans receivable. That evidence was a pastiche of lies and exaggerations, some of them impossible on their face.

By the close of the audit, Templeton was convinced that the figures were ridiculous, but he told no one. Then he was asked to sign a form S-1, an official registration statement filed with the Securities and Exchange Commission, that included the bogus 1968 financial figures. It is a crime knowingly to certify a false SEC statement. For Templeton, the situation became drastic.

In a roomful of his superiors and corporate attorneys, he refused to sign, and left. Someone else signed. A week later, he was called to Goldblum's office. There, Templeton blurted out his suspicion that there was fraud. Goldblum's almond-shaped eyes regarded him coldly. "When are you going to forget all this shit and get to work?" the harsh voice asked.

"Never," said Templeton, and walked out.

Later the same day, Goldblum called him back in and offered him a raise and promotion. Templeton wavered: here was a chance to get places fast, make big money.

Would Goldblum sweeten the pot with more cash, maybe grant Templeton stock options? Sure, said Goldblum. The controller succumbed.

However, he was still deeply disturbed. Ambition at war with conscience, Templeton talked with his wife. One night very soon after that, he went into Goldblum's empty office and left a letter of resignation on the massive, spotless desk. He walked away, one of the few men at Equity Funding who had been exposed to complicity in the fraud and then struggled free of it.

"Never underestimate Goldblum," said Rodney Loeb, general counsel of Equity Funding then and now, and uninvolved in the fraud. "He was a cold man, but a damn good psychologist. He knew just how far to push people and just when to give them a pat on the back. He'd say, 'Give that guy two attaboys and he'll do fine,' and he'd be right." Goldblum even had "attaboy" certificates printed to award to deserving employees.

Templeton's successor as controller was a former auditor, Samuel Lowell, a round, soft dumpling of a man who loved rich living and tournament bridge. His highest qualification for the job, however, lay in his disregard for the niceties his predecessor had observed. Quickly becoming acquainted with the fraud, he fell into it with no discernible struggle and became one of its key operators; before long he was executive vice president for finance and operations, one of Goldblum's closer associates and a principal juggler of the books.

Among other things, Lowell helped in the foreign phase, one of the most ludicrous aspects of the whole conspiracy. Through a series of deals involving shell corporations, phony notes signed by fictitious people like "Dr. Heinrich Wangerhof" and "Alphonso Perez da Silva" (names invented by Goldblum and Lowell), the conspirators tried to raise cash abroad in the form of loans.

The loans never would be recorded as liabilities. The proceeds would be used as 'free credits' to reduce the outrageously large funded-loan figures swelling on the books, and to meet operating expenses. Though the figures showed it was making money, the company all along was losing heavily, and salaries, rents, agents' commissions, vendors, all had to be paid in hard dollars. The foreign operations also served as a maze in which to generate and conceal more bogus income.

Overall, the whole foreign venture was more trouble than it was worth, and only betrayed the amateurish fumbling of its perpetrators. The apogee was reached in 1970 when they tried to swindle the Pope in the purchase of a rundown Rome spaghetti factory, 93 percent of which was owned by the Holy See. They bought it for a song and got the promise of a $5 million loan at low interest to renovate the place, plus another $1.2 million in loan money up front. The latter they quickly shunted into Equity Funding's coffers and, through a complicated series of maneuvers, repatriated most of the rest of the loan, the proceeds of which were to have stayed in Italy to pay for renovation work. The company then went about mismanaging the pasta plant, losing hundreds of thousands of dollars before it was able to unload it. Italian authorities launched criminal investigations centering on the loans, and Equity Funding had to repay them. The whole thing was a typical bungle. With fine scorn, the report of Equity Funding's trustee in bankruptcy concludes that the conspirators "became entranced by a romantic self-image as captains of international business and finance."

While all this was going on, Equity Funding was getting deeper into the business of underwriting insurance. The company's first acquisition, in 1967, was Presidential Life Insurance Company of Illinois, a smallish insurer that was quickly renamed Equity Funding Life Insurance Company (EFLIC) and moved to Los Angeles. With Presidential, Equity Funding purchased the services of its thirty-year-old general counsel, Fred Levin.

Almost immediately, Levin was named president of

EFLIC and became an executive vice president of the parent company in charge of all insurance and marketing operations. (Equity Funding later purchased two other insurers, both untouched by the fraud.) Before long Levin would replace Lowell as Goldblum's right hand, and would corrupt EFLIC thoroughly. He did so with such charm that to this day most of the people he sucked in feel kindly toward him. Many detested Lowell—and at least one referred to him as a "pompous ass"—but they still call Levin "Freddie."

If Levin was a corrupter, he was also corrupted, the victim of a mass of insecurities whose cumulative effect was to drive him unmercifully to achieve. He climbed for the sake of climbing, a mountaineer on a slope whose summit he could never reach or even see. Conscience, a moral structure, anything that might stand in the way, was ground to rubble by this remorseless need to achieve. He was Sammy Glick with warmth.

Like Goldblum, Levin was a Jew, but a practicing, Orthodox Jew. As the son of a poor kosher butcher in Chicago, Levin, like his new boss, had to make his own success and did. President of this class and that student council, a brilliant student in Hebrew theology, an honor student in law school, a bright, energetic young lawyer, he pushed and strove. "I always used everything I had," he says.

So Levin became Goldblum's protege. The chief executive unbuttoned himself more with Levin, and to some extent Lowell, than with anyone else at the company, cracking jokes and holding long, easy conversations. Levin loved it, loved going to Goldblum's house with Lowell, staying up till midnight hatching new plots. He basked in the radiance of Goldblum's regard.

By his own account, he desperately needed that regard. As a boy he remembered his father pacing the floor night after night, harried by fear that his little shop—"a disgusting business," Levin calls it—would fail, that he could not handle the work. Levin was embarrassed by his father's ignorance of English and slipped books under his pillow at night. He was shamed by what he saw as his father's weakness, and frightened by it. Once, says Levin, his father tried to overdose on pills and had to be taken to the hospital. "Another time," he recalls, "I caught him in front of the oven with the gas on."

There was no warmth between them. Gnawed by his anxieties, the elder Levin had no time for his son. "I could never figure out why he didn't play with me, like the other fathers. . . . I remember him as a weak man," Levin says. Freddie Levin would be as different from his father as he could. He would put a world between himself and the butcher shop and that weak and worried man, endlessly pacing the floors at night while the boy listened.

And so it happened. Levin rose, earning a reputation as an honest, diligent young attorney at the Illinois state insurance department, getting hired in 1964 as assistant vice president and general counsel of Presidential when still in his mid-twenties. He worshipped his boss—"I was like his child"—sopping up the attention and affection he never had as a child. In 1968, he became the boss. At thirty he was, he says, the youngest president of any large life-insurance company in the United States. "A real ego trip," Levin says.

Goldblum had made it so. His new young president owed him a lot and knew it. There was a stronger bond. "Maybe I saw Stanley as the father I'd never had," Levin says. "I really liked the guy and felt he liked me. He epitomized everything I ever wanted. He had a big house in Beverly Hills and drove a maroon Rolls-Royce. We were both from the ghetto and worked our way out." Levin was later to do anything necessary to keep the regard and affection of this man Goldblum, who was many things but who certainly was not weak.

But Goldblum's affection alone was not enough, not nearly. Levin had to get it from everywhere he could.

"Fred mother-henned everyone in sight," says general counsel Loeb, who saw him often. "He gave off warmth, because he needed the adulation that came back to him in return. One year, on his birthday, he must have gotten thirty or forty presents from the sales force. He brought me in and waved his arm around and said, "Look at that! Look at how those guys love me." And he kept all that stuff in his office for ten days."

In time Loeb, who was fond of Levin, would wonder whether the young executive had the emotional stability to handle his job. Once Levin rode with Loeb in a limousine after a meeting with officers of Bankers National Life Insurance Company, which Equity Funding purchased in 1971. Levin had been at his best, asking penetrating questions, holding forth at length on insurance matters and Equity Funding's handling of its business, loosening things up with jokes. In the car he was euphoric to the edge of mania. "Those people loved me!" he said. "Didn't I wow them? Didn't I have them eating out of my hand?"

Loeb was told that Levin was certainly up to his job, a brilliant executive who just happened to have "insecurity problems." Don't worry about it, Loeb was told. Still, Loeb did worry. He would sit in meetings with Levin, watching the dark-haired, bespectacled young man gnaw on his fingernails until they were bloody.

On taking over Presidential, Levin surrounded himself with the brightest young executives he could find. He wanted subordinates who were under thirty, younger than himself. He wanted the respect and affection from junior men that he himself had been giving to his seniors. For a man like Levin, giving orders to an older man would be difficult. And how much love, warmth and loyalty could he expect from such a subordinate?

His recruiting was successful. Not long after he took over he was encircled by youngsters. One of them was Lawrence Grey Collins, then twenty-nine, who joined EFLIC as an underwriting manager in 1968. "I was happy where I was before," Collins recalls, "and I didn't want to make a change. Fred asked me out to dinner and I said what the hell, why not listen anyway? So I took my wife along— she's my business manager—and Levin was just a hell of a salesman. He could make you believe things were going to happen, and he told me he was going to make a giant out of the company. This appealed to me and I signed on."

Collins got $15,000, a $3,000 increase from his previous salary. Soon he would become a vice president in charge of all underwriting, and eventually he would earn $30,000 a year and a stock bonus. Collins still felt that much of the time he was underpaid, and he was right. It was a small price to pay for his soul.

Only a few months after Collins came aboard, Levin ordered him to Chicago to sack about thirty employees on the underwriting staff. All the work was being transferred to Los Angeles, and Levin wanted fresh faces, hired locally. Quiet and conservative, Collins was ill-suited for hatchet work, and he quailed. "I could hardly face up to it," he recalls. "It was so shitty, right before Christmas. I had my assistant do most of it. This gave me my first inkling that maybe they might someday be just as cold-blooded with me."

Collins had caught his first glimpse of something cold and ugly that lay under Levin's warmth and candor. Levin did not quail at firing people, far from it; he sometimes seemed to get a perverse joy in it, and he made it a game. Once, when he and another Equity Funding executive went to New Jersey to fire a flock of Bankers National Life employees, Levin toyed with the idea of leaking word that if an employee were summoned to the unmarked office he, Levin, would occupy, the employee would be sacked; but if sent to the colleague's office, the employee would be praised and retained. Then, Levin suggested, the two of them should switch offices, and employees expecting rewards would be fired, and those expecting firing would be rewarded. Levin did drop the cruel hoax. But on another occasion, he told a Bankers executive that a new man was joining the firm. "In whose capacity?" the executive asked. "Yours," Levin said, brutally and truthfully.

No one saw this ugliness at first. EFLIC was humming, relocating and restaffing. By all accounts, it was a grand place to work, completely unlike the tightly ordered, dull gray world of most insurance companies. James Banks, a twenty-nine-year-old lawyer who was hired by Levin in 1968 as counsel and assistant secretary at EFLIC, remembers it fondly.

"The appeal of EFLIC at first was the same thing that kept me there till the end," he says. "Levin's ability to galvanize and lead people was remarkable. The management at EFLIC was a nucleus of young guys intensely loyal to Fred. He promised a lot and delivered a lot. He made it a company with no hours. No one chewed you out for coming in late, and no one patted you on the head for working overtime. It was your time and your company, and there was no rigid hierarchy."

The youth movement overcame EFLIC and the parent Equity Funding as well. Lowell, moving up to an executive vice presidency at thirty, took on a young assistant named Michael Sultan. Later, as controller, Sultan would serve as Lowell's rubber stamp—writing the figures on phony transactions, and doctoring the books at the boss's order. Art Lewis, a brilliant young actuary who became a primary cog in the conspiracy, signed on. So did Lloyd Edens, EFLIC treasurer, later vice president of the parent company. All were on the near side of thirty. And, like many other colleagues just a few years older, they shared a common fate.

All of them would go to jail.

The stress placed upon youth in this management cadre struck some of its former cadremen as an important factor in the success of the fraud. "We were all just crazy, punk kids, really," said Larry Collins. "Our people were easily led: we were too young to have developed mature ethical judgments. I have to wonder if the youth movement wasn't deliberate: In the Army, it's always the young troopers you get to do your killing."

But back then, it wasn't the Army; it was Camelot. There was Levin, giving everybody strokes and getting them in return from his young Turks. Lawyer Banks was caught up in the freewheeling approach and impressed by the glamour of it all.

"If there was a problem, you got on an airplane and you went and solved it," he recalled. Banks, a Canadian newly naturalized as an American, had worked as an obscure tax specialist, the stuffiest of fields, in one of the stuffiest big old-line law firms in Los Angeles. Now he was somebody.

"I would go to all the meetings and conventions and bask in all the compliments we were getting on our growth," he said. "The travel, the compliments—it was all pretty appealing. EFLIC was like the new little kid on the block, trying to make a name for himself. The company was terribly PR conscious, terribly sensitive to how others regarded it."

But at the top of the Equity Funding pyramid, there was trouble. Goldblum kept demanding that earnings per-share grow year by year and quarter by quarter; the stock price had to be supported. But as we have seen, the books were a shambles, the foreign fraud was a botch and there was simply not enough real cash coming in.

Still, no one outside suspected a thing. Wall Street, in the throes of the final surge of the bull market of the sixties, had put a value of $80 a share on Equity Funding stock in 1969. If you had wanted to buy the company for cash on the counter, you would have had to pay about $420 million for its 5.2 million shares of stock; when it had gone public only five years before, it had sold a modest 100,000 shares at only $6 apiece.

But to keep the ball rolling, the company had to have cash to pay its bills. Conventional debt financing was a limited answer. Equity Funding already was borrowing heavily and there were two problems with that; you had to pay interest, and sooner or later you had to pay off the principal. For a company whose real operations were actually losing money all along, the disadvantages in honest borrowing were obvious.

So the management decided to steal. There was no comprehensive plan. Like everything else, this aspect of the fraud, in the words of Equity Funding's trustee, developed in a "helter-skelter, hand-to-mouth" fashion and was preceded by the usual rain dance of rationale, justification and circumlocution.

It was a matter of putting a tentative toe in the water, then wading a little deeper—and finally swimming for your life. The full weight of this part of the fraud fell on Fred Levin and his men at EFLIC.

By now Levin knew about the funding operation. His friend Lowell had told him and Levin's first reaction was, "Hey, Sam—that's *your* problem." But when his turn came, there was no way Levin could thus dismiss Stanley Goldblum.

In 1963, when Equity Funding was just an agency selling insurance policies underwritten by others, it made a pact with Pennsylvania Life Company. In it, Equity Funding agreed, with two minor exceptions, to sell only insurance underwritten by Penn Life, and the latter agreed that only Equity Funding would be its agent in peddling life insurance in conjunction with mutual-fund shares. But Equity Funding's hunger for growth soon left it dissatisfied: the selling part of the insurance business isn't nearly as profitable as the underwriting of coverage, and Equity Funding consequently bought Presidential (later EFLIC). But it was still bound by the Penn Life pact. To get out of it, Equity Funding had to promise that it would resell Penn Life some of the insurance that EFLIC would write—$250 million worth (in face amount) in the 1968-70 period.

Swindled!

This was what the industry calls a reinsurance treaty. It has its legitimate uses. A company may be short of operating cash or the required assets to back the sale of more policies. By selling some off to another insurer, it gets the cash it needs. The buying company is responsible for maintaining the cash reserves to back up the insurance policies it has agreed to underwrite; in return, it should get the lion's share of future premiums.

The policyholder never knows that he has been bartered away to somebody else. The seller company remains responsible for all the bookkeeping and records on the policy and still does all the billing, collecting, and communicating with the insured. The seller also gets to count the policies it has sold as insurance in force, even though the buyer counts them too.

Reinsurance is one of the most poorly regulated activities in an industry where regulation is often abysmally bad anyway. It is largely a gentleman's agreement: the buyer gets from the seller not the actual policies themselves, but just a printout of numbers and other bare data on the policies—premium, type of insurance, and so on. Ordinarily, he simply takes it for granted that he is being dealt with honestly.

When a selling company cedes a policy, it will turn over the annual premium to the buyer. The latter pays the seller an initial amount greater than that premium. This reflects reimbursement of the seller's sales expense and a cut of the profit that accrues when the policy has remained in force for some years.

In its reinsurance deals, Equity Funding got 180 to 190 percent. For every $100 in premium it turned over, essentially, it was getting a quick gross profit in cash of $80 to $90; the long-term profit would go to the reinsurance company that bought the premiums.

After making its deal with Penn Life, a wildly optimistic Equity Funding management also entered into reinsurance agreements with several other concerns. Everyone just assumed that Equity Funding's hot-shot salesmen would drum up enough new life insurance business to meet the Penn Life commitment and more, but early in 1968 it was apparent that they weren't going to come close. This would be embarrassing to a company that was tooting its own trumpet within the industry and up and down Wall Street.

It would also be expensive. Equity Funding's stock might be seriously affected. In addition, the company might also lose an increasingly valuable Penn Life stock option given it as an inducement for sales back in 1965, exercisable now only if the company was able to meet the terms of its Penn Life reinsurance treaty. What to do?

In 1968, the company stuck its corporate toe in the water by issuing what it called "special class" insurance to its own salesmen and employees. At first, they'd be given a big inducement, a 50 percent reduction in the first year's premium, to sign up for coverage on themselves, their wives, children, cousins, great-aunts, and any other relatives they could scrape up. As fast as the business was written it would be dealt off to Penn Life, which would not be told of its "special class" nature.

Then Equity Funding added another inducement. It gave insurance away, completely forgiving the first-year premium. Employees jumped at it, loading up on $50,000 policies for themselves and wives and $25,000 on each of their children, and the business was force-fed to an unsuspecting Penn Life.

The "special class" was, of course, garbage. It would lapse at a sky-high rate the second year, because employees would then have to pay premiums they couldn't have afforded in the first place. The buyer, Penn Life, would be stuck. No one cried about that, says a former EFLIC executive. "People would laugh out loud about it," he said. "They thought it was funny as hell to jab another company that way."

Equity Funding's director of communications and advertising, Gary Beckerman, had a pretty good idea that the special-class business was, to say the least, sharp dealing. But like so many others, the young PR-marketing man rationalized it. "I asked myself, 'Is it honorable?' No. 'Who's hurt?' The reinsurers. 'Is the reinsurer a big boy?' You bet. In the end, I certainly wasn't enthusiastic about it, but it didn't seem worth quitting for. 'Let the country club boys fight it out,' I said, 'I'm just taking my pictures and putting out my releases.' " Beckerman signed his mother up for the special-class coverage. She flunked the physical.

Among the Levin cadre at EFLIC, the special-class ploy went down without anyone gagging. At this stage, anything that helped EFLIC was applauded as inherently desirable. Already, the difference between honest achievement and a reputation founded on lies was blurred; before long it would disappear entirely, and the conspirators would wallow in self-delusion so acute that it bordered on clinical psychosis.

"I had a tremendous amount of corporate loyalty then," said Jim Banks, EFLIC's young counsel. "The company was like your family, like the Mafia. When you spoke you fell into phrases like 'the company and I' and 'me and the company.' You might criticize something internally, but you would never, never badmouth the company to outsiders."

Levin, who hadn't yet taken over EFLIC, had only a peripheral part in the early "special class" scheme, which would continue in 1969 and 1970. But in 1969 he was called on to pay his dues. The men at the top concluded that the potential for special class was too limited to help the company meet the Penn Life quota that year, the company's earnings target, or its need for cash. So Levin and his men designed and operated the so-called "pending business" caper to supplement it.

In this scheme, policies that had been applied for but not yet granted, were recorded as if they were in force and the premiums paid. Then they were sold to Penn Life and others for cash. "Stanley and I came to accept that others were doing the same thing," says Levin. " 'Everybody does it,' we said. But we weren't taking into account the scale of the thing." Up to $750,000 in premiums were sold.

Pending business is also garbage. A high percentage of applications never became policies: applicants strong-armed into applying by salesmen often change their minds, and others can't pass the physical examination, credit check, or other screening measures. The "policies" sold on these dropouts are thus entirely bogus. The company had moved from the resale of real insurance on real people, to insurance of dubious worth on its own employees, to fake insurance on real people. The next step was only natural—fake insurance written on fake people.

In the summer of 1970, the conspirators decided to take that fateful step which has given the most notoriety to the Equity Funding case. They would insure phantoms.

The year 1970 was shaping up as rotten. The company had just made another costly error in judgment dictated by the swollen corporate ego, moving from a Beverly Hills location into its luxurious and expensive new quarters in Century City, quickly dubbed "the Taj Mahal." though the young managers around Levin at EFLIC fancied themselves part of a "hot" company, the hard fact was that the sales force—upon which everything really depended—was falling on its face.

It wasn't all their fault: a recession was dampening new sales and causing policyholders in existing funded pro-grams to drop out as the value of their mutual fund shares fell. Flying high at more than $80 just the year before, Equity Funding's own stock had been clawed in the bear market and had slipped to a historic low of $12. Goldblum was edgy.

The conspirators were also grappling with one of the boomerang effects of reinsuring the special-class and pending business. As expected, special-class policies were lapsing in wholesale lots. Employees were unwilling or unable to pay their full premiums in the second year, and many of the pending policies were never issued. Penn Life smelled a rat and demanded additional reinsurance—but insurance that would stick.

To keep enough business on the books to lull the reinsurers, Equity Funding had to pay the second-year premiums on a sizeable proportion of the garbage. To get the money, and to feed more operating cash into what essentially was an insolvent firm, Goldblum, Levin, Art Lewis and a couple of others felt they had to traffic in phantoms.

This was more than just colossal chutzpah. According to the rules of math, it was suicidal. The company would get a lot of up-front cash when it sold policies, but then would have to hand over all subsequent premiums to the reinsurer for years afterward. Since there would be no live premium payers, the company would have to come up with the money itself. The more it sold in one year, the greater the sum it would have to pay the next. It would have to geometrically increase bogus sales year by year just to stay even.

The actuaries, CPAs and insurance experts involved should have seen this and probably did, but by now everyone was out of touch with reality. Levin recalls convincing himself that he could work the company out of the fraud, that it was only a temporary expedient. "I thought I was Superman," says Levin, who had never before failed at anything.

Even deep into the insurance fraud, the conspirators would refuse to acknowledge its criminality. It was just a way to borrow money interest-free; a loan, as it were, that would be repaid when Equity Funding realized its manifest destiny and started *really* to outsell everyone else in the industry. So the managers said, often enough to persuade themselves.

That they were felons was too much to face squarely, too much for men who, by and large, still regarded themselves as decent, law-abiding citizens. Young Gary Beckerman, the PR-marketing man, was called into Goldblum's office in 1972 and asked to help in the counterfeiting of $100 million in corporate bonds needed to give EFLIC some "assets" it was supposed to have but didn't. "I couldn't, didn't, ever use the word counterfeiting, even to myself," he recalls. "I couldn't have it in my vocabulary. I couldn't apply it to myself." Overpowered by Goldblum, Beckerman went along. Others who did the same found it just as difficult to use words like fraud and forgery.

In late 1970, the company began selling its first blocks of bogus policies, dummied up from altered versions of real ones in force. At the end of the year its reported sales were staggering. EFLIC had almost tripled its insurance in force within twelve months, writing a total of nearly nineteen thousand policies with a face amount of more than $828 million. The industry was agog. The conspirators loved it.

Jim Banks says, "Levin would take enormous pride in having the rest of the industry praise us. I'd come back from meetings and conventions, and he'd always ask what they were saying about us. I'd tell him they were full of admiration for our growth, and he'd just beam. And so would I, so would I. Both of us knew that half or more of the business was fake, but we were honestly, really *proud* anyway. God, what a crazy thing, what self-delusion! When we passed $1 billion in force we took out big ads, and we were proud of them, too."

Lies had become truth; pipedreams, reality. Nasty problems, however, intruded on the dreamers. For one thing, EFLIC was being audited not by good old Wolfson Weiner, who handled the parent company, but by Haskins & Sells. As a matter of course, these auditors would ask for policy files to check against a sampling of the policy numbers EFLIC claimed to have in force. And the many phantom policyholders had no files.

What the conspirators did, in the main, was wait for the auditors to request certain policy files and then, at nighttime "fraud parties" feverishly forge sets of files for delivery to the auditors. This involved filling out medical forms, policy applications, credit checks and other documentation for each policy issued. Later, when the bogus policies were created in huge numbers, a separate "mass marketing" office staffed by young women would whip out forged documents in assembly-line fashion.

When lawyer Banks first was asked to help out at the "parties," he says, it was like "someone asking you to help move a sofa from here to there. I didn't think anything of it; it was something the company needed done, that's all."

Banks' loyalty had lulled his conscience. That loyalty, he feels now, stemmed from gratitude. In his previous job, working as a tax drudge for the starchy Los Angeles law firm, he was waiting to pass the California bar examination and get a job with more pay and more status at the same firm. He passed the examination, but the job offer he got was disappointing.

Banks had gone to law school in his native Canada. The school had little lustre. "I saw that the people the firm was hiring came from the prestigious U.S. schools," Banks says. "I just wasn't in the club." Bearing those scars of rejection, he left for Equity Funding. "I had a lack of confidence," he says. "Deep down, I thought I would never be able to make it if I went into practice for myself, so I felt I owed a lot to the company that had taken me in." Later, he proved himself wrong. Waiting to be indicted, he started his own law practice, and earned about as much from it as he had earned at Equity Funding.

Underwriter Collins was sucked into the forgery for different reasons. Unlike some of the others, he wasn't power-mad, nor was he lusting after high position and a six-figure salary. His profile at the parent company was low—"sort of a Clark Kent," said one executive—and he was seldom seen there. His idea of success was a decent, interesting job that would allow his family to live comfortably, not sumptuously; about $30,000 a year would do it, he figured. He also had no particular loyalty to Equity Funding per se, and had been sufficiently upset at EFLIC's sales of garbage to reinsurers to complain to Levin and threaten to quit.

Collins too, had his insecurities and weaknesses. He had never finished college, and at EFLIC he was in fast company. "I always felt I had to make up for my lack of a degree by sheer effort. I worked my tail off," he says.

A man who labors that hard is usually proud of his work and that of his subordinates, and Collins was. His professionalism was offended by the mess the other conspirators were making of the policy files; as chief underwriter, that was *his* field. Even now there is a hint of outrage in his voice at the sloppy work his colleagues were doing.

"They were just botching it," he complains. "They would have gotten caught without me. They *needed* me; I knew those files and I knew what was supposed to be in them."

Finally, Collins was an eminently agreeable man. He tried to put himself in Levin's shoes, giving careful consideration to the argument that the bogus business was a distasteful but only temporary measure, that it would all be cleaned up and no one would be hurt. In the end, he became a forger too.

"I know I should have just quit on the spot," he says. "My assistant would have, no doubt about it; he was a black-and-white man. I'm very much afraid that I was a shades-of-gray man. . . ."

So it rolled out, cascades of computer printouts laden with phony policies, earnings still rising. A pharaoh perched on the twenty-eighth floor, the top of his Century City headquarters, Goldblum curtly gave his orders. The princelings dancing attendance on him passed the word down to overseers like Banks and Collins directing the serfs who were building Goldblum's treasure city.

The chief executive and to a lesser extent the princelings, were the only people benefiting hugely. They had the really big salaries, stock bonuses, entertainment allowances and perquisites. The lower-level conspirators were rewarded more generously than their honest colleagues, but not by much. Basically, they were putting their necks in the noose to enrich Stanley Goldblum, the principal stockholder. Despite this, at first none of these ill-rewarded overseers even looked up from his desk, not even Collins. By now, he knew that what he was doing was criminal, and he knew his world would be shattered by any disclosure of the scandal.

He was terribly afraid, but kept plowing blindly on, out of some mistaken notion of loyalty. "If I'd had the brains," he marvels, "I would have said, 'What the hell are we doing? The guys upstairs are raping us.'" But though he threatened to quit several times, Collins could not break away.

The fraud was dragging more bodies into its vortex. One belonged to Alan Green, a twenty-four-year-old trainee working for chief actuary Art Lewis, described by one conspirator as "a brilliant man with a truly sinister mind." Early in 1972, Lewis invited Green to his home for drinks and dinner; they both got drunk and Lewis spilled the crucial elements of the insurance fraud to his young assistant, asking him to help program phony policies into the data-processing system.

Lewis probably didn't realize it, but he could not have picked a more likely recruit for the fraud. "My first reaction was surprise but not shock," Green admits. "I thought to myself, 'Far out! This is really something.' And I was flattered that I was being asked in. Lewis said that he and Edens specifically were trying to become more important within the company, and the way they were doing it was to build up the size of EFLIC. 'We're on a power trip,' he said."

Green himself was on no power trip. He considered corporate life a hideous bore and he rejected its values. He was little interested in money; his payoff for joining the fraud was a raise that amounted to a grand total of $600 before he quit to roam about the country in a van. The only thing that personally interested him in the fraud was an opportunity to do computer programming. He thought that might be intellectually stimulating.

There was something else. Nonconformist as he was in many areas, Green still retained much of the good soldier, and his new assignment was partly just a matter of obeying orders. "I've noticed since then that my attitude toward my superiors has always been one of respect and a little fear," he says. "It's been my attitude toward my teachers, toward my bosses, toward my supervisor in prison. That was part of it."

And Green also, by his own account, had a definite criminal tendency. "I was—am—a self-centered person," he observes. "The foremost thing on my mind was whether or not this thing was right for me—not other people, me. If I'd thought there was a big chance I'd be caught, I wouldn't have done it. But I didn't see myself getting indicted. I should have known better."

Indeed. Green, a good student, used to cheat on tests anyway. He always got caught. As a child, he stole things. He got caught. After he left Equity Funding, he drifted into a job at a bookstore, and found a way to steal. Nailed again, he was fired.

Green signed on without giving a thought to the morality of the thing. The day after his talk with Lewis he was helping forge policy files. It amused him. One corporation's ripping off others tickled his sense of irony, as it did that of some other participants. "Party is a good term for it," he says. "There was a lot of hilarity. Everybody wanted to be the doctor." Between parties, Green programmed the phony business into the computer. Iconoclastic, drugged with LSD much of the time, he certainly was one of the most offbeat of the fraud participants.

Phantom policyholders have one unhappy attribute, aside from their absolute inability to pay their own insur-

71

ance premiums. They live forever, and thus owe premiums forever, unless you can murder them. In 1971, Equity Funding began to murder its phantoms. It started filing forged death claims with reinsurers who had purchased the bogus policies. The reinsurers would forward the insurance payoff to Equity Funding. Having no widow or orphan to turn the money over to, the company kept it. The scheme accelerated vastly in 1972, and early in 1973 Levin decided to kill $10 million worth of phantom policyholders. He was finally persuaded that this genocide surely would be remarked by the reinsurers; $3 million or so seemed more reasonable.

Banks was a principal architect and operator of the death-claim procedure, and before long he was diverting some of the proceeds into his own pocket. How could Banks, the company loyalist, do it? The atmosphere at EFLIC and the parent company was changing. A moral infection had become gangrenous, and Levin was removed from day-to-day contact with his followers, spending most of his time above them on the twenty-eighth floor.

That the underlings were risking their freedom for the men on that floor and getting little for it, became apparent at last. Morale plunged. Greed and fear took over. Gradually the company was riddled with subcells of conspirators and lone-wolf operators stealing everything they could while there was still something left to steal.

First Banks, then Edens, Lewis and another employee, were taking death-claim money for themselves from reinsurers. Then they took it from EFLIC itself. Then they stole checks. Another subcell rigged the computer to pay its members unauthorized commissions. A lone wolf tried to make off with the cash values of lapsed policies. The executives were running wild; one triple-billed his expense accounts, another had the company pay for his divorce, another furnished a girlfriend's apartment, courtesy of Equity Funding.

"There wasn't any talk of corporate loyalty anymore,"

says Banks. "Nobody cared, there wasn't a shred of morality left. The whole structure was rotten to the core." Earlier, when Frank Majerus, EFLIC's controller, became deeply troubled by the fraud and consulted his minister, he was told to get out of the company; when he gave this news to his colleagues, he was derided. "When Majerus said that, well, we just roared," Banks says. "It seemed so laughable then. It was only much later we realized how lucky he'd been to have someone help pull him out of it." Majerus finally did quit and escaped jail.

Few were that fortunate. The fraud had slowly been isolating the conspirators, cutting them off from friends, churches, and even their own wives.

"The company, the fraud, was taking the place of the marital relationship," says Banks. Always close to his wife, they temporarily drifted apart during the period of the swindle. Terrie Collins complained that Larry was never at home; where *was* he all those nights? It took a lot of convincing to prove to her that he was indeed putting in eighty hours a week in Goldblum's vineyard. A former deacon in his church, Collins could not spare the time for it anymore and Levin, the Orthodox Jew, was neglecting temple. Disclosure of the fraud would shatter Levin's marriage entirely.

Collins, on the thin edge now, looked for someone to tell who could give him objective advice. There was no one, no family close by, no friends who weren't in the insurance business. He was alone.

He could discuss it with none of his subordinates, instinctively knowing it might be fatal to expose them to the corruption of the fraud. He did not want them to drink from the same cup that had already poisoned him. So he lied to them or told them nothing. Once he deliberately passed over for promotion a man he knew had a good outside offer, thus forcing him away from Equity Funding. The man was hurt—until the scandal broke. He then thanked Collins for his kindness.

By late 1972, the dread that the whole thing could blow

anytime was pervasive. Caught by Goldblum and Levin in the embezzlement scheme, Banks and others were told to repay the money and some were given stock bonuses to help them do so. Goldblum, said Banks, appealed to them to stay and "save the stockholders."

It didn't escape their attention that this really meant, in large part, "save Goldblum." But they knew there were thousands of other people involved, too. Their own careers and the security of their families were also on the line. Alan Green says: "The one thing they couldn't afford to do then was just stop."

The younger executives, however, did get a grudging commitment from Goldblum to at least try to put on the brakes. Thus was born "Project Z," the ineffectual attempt to gradually get out of the bogus insurance spiral before it was too late. One of the first moves was an attempt to slash company costs deeply, and it proved to be the final, fatal error.

One of those let go in early 1973 for economy reasons was Ronald Secrist, who knew of the fraud and had been a minor participant in it at one time, and who had been packed off to work at Bankers Life when he became queasy. Smarting at his dismissal, Secrist got himself another job and then made a couple of phone calls, one to a rumpled, inquisitive little securities analyst named Ray Dirks, a specialist in insurance stocks, and the other to insurance regulators.

There had been suspicion and minor leaks before, but for the first time the code of *omerta* that had kept present and former employees from talking had been breached in a significant way. This silence of almost nine years had its roots in fear; by and large, the people who had any concrete, first-hand knowledge of the fraud were people who already had been soiled by it. If they talked, they feared, they would find themselves in trouble immediately.

Others knew of the fraud, but all their knowledge was hearsay. They had heard oblique references to what was

going on, or specifics about one area of the fraud. But they
themselves had seen nothing and done nothing; they could
not be absolutely certain. Still others had seen or done
some minor things they considered improper or unusual,
but had been boxed off from information about the entire
nature of the conspiracy; all they would have to talk about
were what appeared to be minor improprieties. So, until
Secrist, there was silence.

In mid-March of 1973, insurance examiners for the states
of California and Illinois (the official home state of Presidential, then EFLIC) suddenly appeared at EFLIC's
offices. They said it was a routine triennial audit. It was
actually a surprise audit aimed at verifying Secrist's information.

Meanwhile, Dirks had tipped the *Wall Street Journal* to
Secrist's allegations and was poking into some dark corners
himself. Informants began to surface and in late March
began to talk to the SEC as well as the *Journal*. On Wall
Street, big institutions alerted by Dirks began to sell, and
soon big blocks of Equity Funding stock were being tossed
down the street like so many white-hot cannonballs. Prices
on the stock fell from the twenties into the low teens in
days. Trading was halted. Rumors spread; Equity Funding
denied them all.

The conspirators were overwhelmed by shock and panic.
Lewis broke out in a severe skin rash. His hands trembling,
Collins would look in the mirror in the morning and feel a
sick dread at the very thought of going to the job he had
once enjoyed so much. "It was a nightmare," he says. "We
were trapped inside a volcano. We could have talked,
spilled the whole thing, but we would have blown up with
everyone else. It was just too late." Banks, anesthetized
all this time, finally sensed that he had an excellent chance
of going to jail. A couple of months before, when he had
thought of leaving the company, he had for the first time
analyzed what he'd been doing. "I knew then I had con-

fused the illegal part of the company's business with the legal," he says. "There were two channels; one open, honest, regular, the other secretive, illegal, both going on at the same time. I had never separated the two. When you sign on, I told myself, you agree to do the company's business. This was part of the business of the company and I did it." Toward the end, Banks says, he was spending 80 percent to 90 percent of a crushing work week in the dark waters of that second channel. Then Levin asked him to do one final fraudulent thing, and he told his boss to go to hell. But it was too late for him anyway.

In a last attempt to block discovery of the fraud, Goldblum ordered the bugging of the company offices that had been loaned to the insurance examiners, hoping to ferret out their plans. Collins assisted in this ("good old Larry, always ready to help out," he recalls bitterly), stringing wires into the listening post—Goldblum's bathroom. Banks helped too ("morally, it was hideous"), and one day found himself sitting on Goldblum's toilet, listening to the examiners talk while the chief executive coolly entertained company in his office next door.

By Friday, March 30, the examiners had not yet found the bogus policies. But Illinois authorities did discover that $24 million in bonds, the lion's share of EFLIC's claimed assets, had never existed (the plan to use some of the counterfeit bonds never worked; the printing job was bad). The next day, Illinois moved to seize the company and found California had already done so Friday night.

Rodney Loeb, the general counsel, was thunderstruck when it became clear to him that the worst of the rumors, and more, were probably true. Loeb concedes he himself was no businessman—"all I ever wanted to be was a good lawyer"—and he had never dreamed that Goldblum could be involved. In matters involving securities law, Goldblum had ordered that Equity Funding be beyond reproach. Loeb had hired a tough little SEC lawyer named Larry Williams as chief of compliance, and together, at

Goldblum's urging, they prepared guidelines for the conduct of the company's securities salesmen that both considered airtight.

Goldblum was the chairman of a district committee of the National Association of Securities Dealers. When he returned from meetings where unethical sales practices were discussed, Loeb recalled, "he always wanted to know, 'Could it happen here? I don't want it to ever happen' and Larry and I would work on it."

Once, an Equity Funding salesman peddled a funding package, which takes ten years to mature, to an eighty-seven-year-old woman. Williams recommended a stiff punishment, a suspension for sixty days. But Goldblum, outraged, said, "Hell no! We're going to fire the son of a bitch right now!" And they did.

Could this man have pulled off one of the hugest, most audacious frauds in the history of American business? Loeb couldn't believe it—until, that week before the fall, Goldblum hired a lawyer who told him to plead the Fifth Amendment if called before the SEC and advised that his princelings hire themselves the best criminal counsel they could.

Loeb, as secretary of Equity Funding, called an emergency meeting of the board over that fateful last weekend. There was shouting and tumult when Goldblum refused to answer some point-blank questions about what had gone on. His resignation was forced out of him, and after he vainly tried to get severance pay and a $200-a-day consulting post, he, Levin and Lowell were ordered off the premises.

The next day, April 2 1973, the *Wall Street Journal* broke the story on its front page and Equity Funding blew to pieces. Its offices around the country were paralyzed, telephones shut down. Creditors descended on it in swarms; so did policyholders and securities holders. Loeb and another uninvolved executive vice president, Herbert Glaser, were trying to run the company, and it fell to Loeb that Monday to fire the other principal conspirators. Some of them demanded consulting posts, too, on the ground that they were the only ones who could run the company. So far had delusion gone. Loeb offered to throw them out the window.

Mickey Sultan, Lowell's young assistant and rubber-stamp, was different. Getting word later that day from the authorities that he was apparently involved and should be fired, Loeb was pained. He had always liked Sultan. He told him gently, and Sultan only said: "It's all right, Rodney. I understand."

Shortly afterward, Loeb had a chance meeting with Sultan in the company parking garage. "He looked at me and broke down and cried," says Loeb. "I gave him a handkerchief and told him, 'Don't cry. What's done is done; it's over.' And he said, 'Rodney, I'm so sorry to have done this to you, to the others, to have fooled everyone.'"

Nothing short of bankruptcy proceedings could save what was left of the company. On Wednesday, April 4, after helping to prepare the petition that would be accepted by the court the next day, the general counsel went home and sat on the edge of his bed.

He had come to Equity Funding from a job at Commonwealth United Corporation, another Beverly Hills hot-air balloon that had fallen under the weight of its own debentures. Now this. Loeb began to weep. It was the first time his wife had ever seen him cry.

Within three days of the *Journal* story, more than $10 billion worth of civil lawsuits from courts across the country had rained down on Equity Funding and its officers and directors, innocent and guilty alike. Those suits are still pending.

Stripped of most of their executive staff, both EFLIC and the parent firm were in absolute chaos. The SEC recruited and the court approved a trustee to run Equity Funding under protection of Chapter 10 of the Bankruptcy Act. It was the biggest fraud-induced Chapter 10 proceeding in

American business history.

Over months of investigation, the whole sorry story squeezed into the light. Of $3.2 billion in life insurance EFLIC had purportedly written, about two-thirds was pulled out of thin air. Later, the company would be ordered dismantled, and its flesh-and-blood policyholders entrusted to a subsidiary untarred by the fraud.

The parent company, which was supposed to have a net worth of over $143 million, didn't have a net worth at all; whacking down those impossibly bloated assets and adding real but undisclosed liabilities to the books, the trustee found it actually had liabilities that exceeded its assets by more than $40 million. Equity Funding was worse than broke and had been for a long time. Only borrowed and stolen money had kept it going.

For the army of creditors and securities holders, there was precious little. After selling off everything he could, trustee Robert Loeffler would eventually come up with a reorganization plan, now moving toward execution, for a new company centered on the two untouched insurance subsidiaries. In this proposed replay of the miracle of loaves and fishes, the banks and other senior, secured creditors would get some cash and notes payable from the income of the new company. All other claimants would have to settle for new stock in this new company, of undetermined market value.

The common stockholders of Equity Funding would get new shares, worth about twelve cents for each dollar of loss. It isn't much, but then neither was Equity Funding. Trustee Loeffler says the whole story of the fraud reminds him very much of *Alice in Wonderland,* a favorite of his when he was a boy.

Society treats the stock swindler with a tolerance that borders on admiration. The absence of violence in his particular crime tends to defuse antagonism, for one thing.

For another, there is a sneaking delight in all of us at seeing someone outwit the system, however short-lived his success.

The courts reflect this. Dragged before the bar, the stock-fraud artist cuts an appealing figure; well-dressed, well-barbered, well-spoken, represented by the ablest counsel stolen money can buy, he is the embodiment of contrition. This is clearly no surly felon menacing the public safety, but a fellow country-club member who in a moment of weakness strayed from the path and now knows it. Give him a light sentence.

But if punishment is in any way connected with the sheer bulk of suffering that the criminal caused, justice simply isn't being done in many cases. The victims of a major stock fraud may run well into the thousands, and most are not fat cats who can write it off, hop a train for Scarsdale and forget it over cocktails. They are litttle people who bleed and suffer for months and years and perhaps the rest of their lives. In this sense the toll taken by Equity Funding was one of the most horrible of any modern crime.

The day that the news of the fraud broke, Equity Funding stock that had been worth almost $300 million in market value at the beginning of the year was worth zero. The company's bonds and warrants were also suddenly worthless. Among the little people there was consternation, then numbness, and finally a sick pain as the impact of what had happened seeped through. A year after the fraud was unmasked, it was still ruining lives.

On that first anniversary, a seventy-four-year-old widow named Peggy Rahn was sitting in her tiny New York apartment, looking at her bankbook. It said she had $900 left in the world. Her Social Security payments weren't quite enough to cover her rent. Gainfully employed for fifty-five years, always proudly self-sufficient, she was being inexorably pushed toward the welfare rolls. "Every day I wake up and wonder what will happen to me," she said. She wishes she had never ever heard of Equity Funding Corporation of America, in which she invested $7,000—almost all of the money she had.

With the sudden losses came shame, and attempts at secrecy so that loved ones would not learn of what happened and begin to fear for the future. Across the Hudson from Mrs. Rahn's apartment in New York, a New Jersey shopkeeper in failing health yearned for retirement but was still dragging himself to work; his wife and son could not understand why. Self-employed, ineligible for Social Security, he had put more than $25,000, the bulk of his life savings, into Equity Funding securities. His wife and son did not know the company had blown up, and he was hiding it from them. "I don't know how much longer I can do it, but I have to," he said, weeping. "How can I ever tell my wife I lost most of the money we were going to retire on? I don't know what it will do to her, and I'll die of shame."

At the same time, in a small town in Nebraska, a college student who badly needed medical care his parents could not afford had hit on a way to get the needed money. He would sock it into Equity Funding, a hot growth stock. He invested the day before trading was halted. His parents, who borrowed on their home to put up the capital for him, were trying not to let him see how terribly worried they were. His medical treatments were, of course, delayed.

Lynbrook Larry, a retiree, was raging at the regulators. "Where were the men who were supposed to look out for us little people?" he asked. Larry, who went down with $21,000 worth of securities, told his wife but not his friends. "Nobody knows the trouble we're having. Nobody can," he whispered. "It would kill my wife if they knew; she'd commit suicide or something."

There are others, a far greater number, who were victimized and will never know it. They are the potential beneficiaries of various trusts, pension funds and endowments stuck with Equity Funding securities.

Swindled!

To the gentlemen overseeing these mountains of money, the losses they faced were piddling. Princeton University's endowment fund had $1.3 million in Equity Funding, it's true, but it also had about $500 million in things that didn't go broke.

The State Teachers Retirement Fund of Ohio would barely notice a $10.8 million loss. And a $50,000 loss to the trust providing income to the Laughlin Children's Center in Pittsburgh, which treats youngsters with learning disabilities, wasn't fatal.

That is one way to look at it. But it remains that to the extent these investments are losses, the beneficiaries of these funds will be the poorer. The $50,000 was a third of the annual operating budget of the children's center. At the many colleges holding Equity Funding, losses can be translated into faculty salaries and student scholarships. Just how many people will ultimately lose in the Equity Funding debacle, then, will never be known.

Among the hardest-hit groups were the present and former employees of Equity Funding who were innocent of wrongdoing in the fraud. The company's collapse cost most of them their jobs, and the nature of its failure made it difficult for them to find new ones. Other companies were understanding and sympathetic; and in the end, they decided they didn't want the words "Equity Funding" in their personnel records.

General counsel Rodney Loeb and his chief of compliance, Larry Williams, were badly scorched. Just before trading was stopped, Williams urged his brother to invest heavily in Equity Funding stock on behalf of their father. Goldblum had sworn up and down to Williams that absolutely nothing was wrong, so that made the stock a real buy.

Loeb was stuck with $75,000 in loans he had made in order to pay taxes on his stock bonuses. The stock itself was collateral and now its price, in those last days, was dropping steeply. We want to sell you out, the bank said, but

Equity Funding: "I Did It for the Jollies"

Loeb couldn't allow it; under securities law he was an insider, and his right to dispose of stock was limited. After the debacle the bank got nasty, and Loeb had to give it a second mortgage on his home, refinance his first mortgage, sell some possessions and borrow from his family.

He got the debt down to $55,000, and the bank then gave him more time to pay this off. Loeb told his son in New York that he could no longer help him financially. His wife didn't buy a dress and he didn't buy a suit. After two years of pounding and grinding, the tab is now down to about $30,000.

When the scandal exploded in his face, Loeb felt the deepest humiliation. "I avoided every place where I'd be in contact with other lawyers," he recalls. "I felt I would never be able to hold up my head again. People certainly would have snickered behind my back and said, 'Sure, he didn't know.'" This feeling has largely disappeared and Loeb believes he has reestablished himself now in his profession.

But he adds: "It's still painful to face the only two alternatives to the question of how this could have gone on for so long without the general counsel knowing. Either I was very stupid or very naive, or both."

For the conspirators themselves, the span of more than two years between exposure of the fraud and their sentencing seemed interminable. Larry Collins was broke, and had to borrow $5,000 from his mother to pay a lawyer. He fell ill with suspected lung cancer that turned out to be something else, and his wife Terrie had to go in for psychiatric counseling. Fred Levin sold Mazda automobiles for a while and then sank into lethargy, passing endless days reading every word of the *Wall Street Journal* and talking to people on the phone. He and his management cadre were cooperating fully with the investigators. Stanley Goldblum wasn't talking.

Jim Banks remembers sitting in front of his television

set, watching a parade of young presidential aides baring their souls at the Watergate hearings. "I listened to those underlings," he says, "and I found myself sympathizing with them and nodding when they talked. They did what they did in the name of national security, invoked by the President of the United States. Now, my president was just this shithead over in Beverly Hills, I know, but he had us do things in the name of corporate well-being. That was pretty powerful stuff for me then."

The indictments came in November 1973. Eighteen of the men who were charged eventually pleaded guilty. Of the company executives, only Goldblum held out, and even he decided to plead guilty shortly after his trial began in October 1974, following damaging testimony against him by Jerry Evans. Shortly afterward, auditors who had been indicted were convicted after a lengthy trial.

In the spring of 1975 the sentences came down. U.S. Attorney William Keller personally pleaded in court for a twenty-year sentence for Stanley Goldblum as a deterrent to white-collar crime and a fitting punishment. The judge gave him eight years.

Among the others, Levin and Lowell got five years each and Lewis, Edens and Banks, three. Smith, Sultan, and Collins got two years. Green got a two-year suspended sentence; but he had to serve three months, and he was put on probation for three years. Jerry Evans got a year's suspended sentence and probation. Gary Beckerman got two years, suspended, and probation. The accountants later got two-year suspended sentences, three months of actual jail time, and four years probation. They also were required to do 2,000 hours of charity work.

As Levin waited for the day when he would enter prison, he was tormented by dreams. In one he relived a real experience, when a good friend in the securities business who had recently suffered a heart attack told him, only days before trading halted, that he had bought $100,000 worth of Equity Funding stock. "I believe in you," he told

Levin, who knew the man must have gone in debt to make the purchase. "I wanted to tell him to sell right away, but I couldn't, I couldn't," says Levin. "Only his firm and another brokerage house were keeping the stock afloat." The only time Levin has seen or talked to his friend since are in those recurring dreams.

In other dreams, he saw the faces of old people, stockholders, who came to Presidential Life when Equity Funding was going to buy it for stock. They wanted more dividends. "Don't worry," Levin would say in his dreams, "Your stock is going to be replaced by the stock of a wonder growth company." Sometimes, Levin says, he woke in a cold sweat.

Through it all, he could not actually cry over what had happened. But a friend tells how Levin would sit for hours in front of his TV set, watching the old movies of which he is so fond. Then, during the sad parts, he would weep.

The flower fields of Lompoc, California, lie in rainbow bands across a little valley that opens to the sea. The air is heavy with floral perfumes and the tang of the Pacific. About 160 miles north of Century City, Lompoc might as well be on Mars, so far removed is it in spirit and pace from the mindless hustle of the metropolis to the south. Here they raise flowers to make money, or they work at what the Bureau of Prisons calls the "Correctional Facility," a prim euphemism for the federal penitentiary and camp. Petunias are big business here but so is punishment.

If you have to go to jail the camp is not a bad jail to go to. Guards are unarmed, there are trees and lawns, a gym, even a scruffy athletic field and golf course. Khaki-clad inmates look like privates stuck in some boondocks post run by a commanding officer who has let discipline slip a bit.

There are hard cases in the nearby prison, but the camp itself houses gentler felons—bewildered wetbacks and a conglomeration of white-collar criminals. There are bank tellers who withdrew from other people's accounts, bush-league mail fraud artists, politicians who couldn't get their hands out of the cash register in time, perjurers, and a clutch of people who used to work for Equity Funding.

Alan Green, the programmer who plugged the phony policies into EFLIC's computer, likes it here. He has had time to get acquainted with himself and has found there is much he never realized.

He has no remorse over the legions of swindled investors and the others marked by the scandal. "Equity Funding was only one example of a widespread disease," he says. "In that light, what was so wrong with what I was doing? It was only what many others were doing. I didn't see any responsibility on my part for the investors and the others and I don't blame myself now—that just wouldn't do me a bit of good."

But out of sheer self-interest, Green has spent a lot of time thinking about how to avoid what could be called the Finger of God, the force that always seems to come down out of the clouds and squash him whenever he has done something wrong. Internal mechanisms—a sense of morality, a code of ethics—don't mean much to Green. But the seeming inevitability of punishment does.

"The primary thing with me is still what is going to be best for me. I certainly don't want to go to jail again," he says. "Now I'm able to see in myself that criminal tendency to always try to get something for nothing. All the times I tried I was caught. Now that I know I have this tendency, I can control it."

But what if the opportunity to commit a criminal act came again, another chance to get something for nothing, and this time it was *absolutely certain* that Green *couldn't* be caught? A hypothetical question, certainly, but Green considers it seriously. "I think," he says carefully, "that would have to depend on the specific situation."

If Green is reasonably content here, assessing himself

while assembling furniture in the prison factory, for others the experience is nearly unbearable. They suffer from the common but debilitating disease of most men in captivity, "slow time." Every tick of the clock is separated by a gulf from the next; each hour flows as slowly as syrup. And, for all the little niceties of the camp, for all the lack of walls and watchtowers, they are keenly conscious that they have no freedom.

"They try hard here," Larry Collins sighs, "but you can't forget you're in the joint." He passes the time on a landscape crew whose foreman amuses them with tales of *mafiosi,* politicos and businessmen he has had pulling weeds and clipping shrubs under his direction. Collins, like others, lives mainly for visits from his wife, and in the long spaces between, he thinks of why this happened to him.

"I kick myself for being weak," he says. "I never was a real yes man. But I was weak. I still consider myself honest, but I went along with it. I must have *wanted* to believe the things they were telling me. You have to worry about your sense of ethics, of morality, when this happens. I'm a very adaptable person, good old Larry, always ready to listen to the other guy's arguments, and to weigh his point of view. And that's what got me in here."

Jim Banks is resigned to Lompoc. Of his being here, he says, "There are good reasons. I stole a lot of money." But his helplessness to ease the strain on his wife and family constantly discourages him. He may have got what was coming to him, but they are suffering more. "I have three children," he says. "One has a stuttering problem that has gotten much worse. Another is a daughter who was always cheerful, outgoing. Now she's withdrawn into herself. I've got to believe it's because of what's happened, not having her father there."

A lawyer, Banks expects to be disbarred. He isn't quite sure what he will do when he leaves Lompoc, but he has one idea.

Swindled!

"There are a lot of people out there in a lot of companies who will do what I did at Equity Funding," he says. "Somebody has to tell them about priorities, somebody has to tell them what a company and a career mean in the scheme of things, and what place a man's family has. I've been there; I could counsel them. And the first thing I'd say is, 'If it happens, don't think you can stop anytime. You aren't going to be strong enough to extricate yourself. You're going to need help.'"

A guard reminds him that his time is up. He walks across a parking lot and a strip of lawn to the waiting prison barracks.

Is Banks still deluding himself, disguising himself in the company of a herd of thousands or hundreds of thousands of young businessmen who he would have you believe are just as vulnerable to criminality as he was?

Not long ago, an assistant professor of management at the University of Georgia, Archie Carroll, made a survey of some 240 business executives that provides a clue to an answer. Most of the people who responded were middle and lower managers who were insidiously threatened by the expectations of their superiors.

Did they feel under pressure to compromise their personal standards to meet company goals? Sixty-five percent said yes. The lower in the corporate pecking order, the stronger the feeling became; 84 percent of the lower-level managers reported it. Could the respondents conceive of a situation where the managers of the company were ethical men but so demanding of results that there would be compromises of conscience and morality? Yes, said more than 78 percent.

This question was not asked, but it is a natural one: Now what if the chief executive is a Stanley Goldblum, a powerful presence, a dark god on the twenty-eighth floor, who not only wants the bottom line to look good but who prescribes criminal measures to make it so? If the millions of white-collar spear carriers in American business feel threatened by the very authority structure in which they labor, the answer seems clear.

At Ohio State University, Professor Frederick Sturdivant was teaching a class in business ethics. He laid out the Equity Funding case to his students and asked them what they would do had they worked at the company. Even knowing the denouement, an alarming number said they would be, as the professor put it, "good Germans." They would go along.

IV

The Biggest Ponzi Scheme:
A Reporter's Journal
By David McClintick

For eight months during the fall and winter of 1973–74, a reporter's dream story lay buried in voluminous documents in the office of the clerk of the United States District Court in Tulsa, Oklahoma. The papers contained the salient details of the now-familiar Home-Stake Production Company swindle. This was a spectacular fraud, then unknown to American newspaper readers, that had bilked some of the country's most famous entertainers, business executives, political figures and assorted other personalities out of perhaps $100 million or more.

No doubt, the Home-Stake story would have been told at some time, in some newspaper. It was told when it was, in the pages of the Wall Street Journal, *because reporter David McClintick just happened to have lunch one day with a certain New York tax lawyer.*

This chapter is Dave McClintick's own painstakingly reconstructed story behind that story: how he stumbled onto and reported one of the most dramatic cases of fraud ever exposed in America.
—Donald Moffitt

The Biggest Ponzi Scheme: A Reporter's Journal

It was Friday, March 1 1974. A friend and I were to meet for lunch in midtown Manhattan and discuss, not for the first time, a seemingly prosaic but actually intriguing topic—the tax aspects of International Telephone & Telegraph Corporation's merger with Hartford Fire Insurance Company. I had written some articles about it, and my friend, a tax lawyer whom I shall call Paul, had helped me grasp some of the ploys ITT used in getting the Internal Revenue Service to approve the merger, the largest in corporate history.

Only minutes before noon, the Watergate grand jury had returned its long-awaited indictments of Haldeman, Ehrlichman, Mitchell, Colson, Mardian, Parkinson and Strachan. The news flashed across the country. I heard it from a breathless CBS correspondent on a cab driver's radio on the way uptown from Wall Street and it was the first thing Paul and I talked about over lunch.

After also discussing the ITT-Hartford case, Paul said, almost in passing as we parted, "If you ever get tired of ITT, you might want to take a look at a company that's in trouble down in Oklahoma. It's a different kind of situation from ITT and Equity Funding, and the man in the middle of it makes Stanley Goldblum (the convicted mastermind of the Equity Funding fraud) look like a saint."

I asked Paul the name of the company. "Home-Stake," he said. I promptly forgot it. Paul told me something more memorable, however. Walter Matthau and possibly some other show business celebrities had invested in the Oklahoma company and might have lost a lot of money. As far as Paul knew, no other newspapers were aware of the situation.

I was then researching and writing three other important stories for the *Wall Street Journal*. Each had a March or early April deadline, and I didn't seek out Paul again until late one afternoon in the third week of March. Paul was acquainted with a few investors in Home-Stake and had collected several documents bearing on the case:

copies of four lawsuits that had been filed against the company and brief lists of investors, amounting to no more than three or four dozen names.

Sitting at a spare desk in Paul's office suite, I scanned the material closely enough to get the drift of the charges against the company, whose full name turned out to be Home-Stake Production Company. It was a Tulsa-based oil-drilling tax-shelter concern that had raised $100 million or more over several years by projecting that investors would get back three or four times their initial outlay in profits from oil discoveries. Home-Stake also had promised that investors could write off their investments on their tax returns, since oil-drilling investments generally are deductible. According to the lawsuits, the investors had received only a tiny fraction of the returns they had been promised, and the Internal Revenue Service was challenging their tax deductions. The IRS apparently had concluded that most of the money hadn't been spent for drilling, the tax-deductible activity for which it was intended.

Aside from Walter Matthau, who was a plaintiff in one of the suits, the only names I recognized on Paul's lists were Alan Alda, the star of television's "M*A*S*H"; Jack Cassidy, a moderately well-known song-and-dance man who until recently was married to Shirley Jones, and Jack's son, rock singer David Cassidy. It hardly amounted to a "Who's Who of Hollywood"; but Paul said he had heard that Barbra Streisand, Bob Dylan and Buddy Hackett were also investors.

"How did these people get into this?" I wrote in my notebook. The question was obvious, but getting the full answer was to prove very difficult and would consume much of the next three months.

It was past 5:00 P.M. Paul produced a bottle of Johnny Walker Black Label and some ice from the office refrigerator, poured a couple of drinks and proceeded to tell me what else he knew about the Home-Stake case.

The company had been founded by Robert Trippet, a

Tulsa lawyer about fifty-five years old. Trippet had graduated near the top of his class from the University of Oklahoma law school. He was bright and imaginative. Home-Stake, Paul said, was running a "Ponzi scheme." That was a new term to me, and Paul explained what it meant. A Ponzi-scheme operator collects money from investors and uses part of it to pay a "return," encouraging the investors to put more into the venture. Home-Stake had been able to collect increasing amounts each year from 1964, the first year it offered investments publicly, until 1971, when investments began to decline. Apparently the company had spent relatively little of the money drilling for oil. Paul said he understood that out of the $18 million Home-Stake collected in 1970, about $14 million couldn't be accounted for.

Every Ponzi swindler eventually must deal with investors who get disgruntled at lower-than-promised payments. Apparently, Trippet had divided his investors into groups according to their expertise and influence. Those who were astute or powerful enough to cause trouble if they got suspicious were paid relatively well. Those Trippet evaluated as "live ones" were paid little. Or so some investors charged in court.

If an investor complained, Trippet allegedly would offer several plausible reaons why payments weren't larger. If the investor was unsatisfied by the explanation, Trippet would offer to let him trade in his shares for shares in another Home-Stake drilling program. Or Trippet would suggest that the investor donate his shares to charity and take another tax deduction. If the investor was still unhappy, or if he threatened to sue, Trippet sometimes agreed to refund his investment. Home-Stake's drilling shares, known as "participation units" in its drilling programs, were distinct from the common stock that the company also issued.

The most bizarre tale Paul had heard dealt with some California farm land where Home-Stake was drilling for oil. Actually it had done very little drilling, but the company had painted several irrigation pipes bright pink and orange and put coded markings on them to make it appear that the pipes carried Home-Stake oil production.

Paul had no idea what had happened to the bulk of the money Home-Stake raised but hadn't spent for drilling. He did mention that Trippet allegedly devised one scheme to funnel about $3 million from Home-Stake into his own pocket.

The next day I looked up Home-Stake Production Company in the *Journal* files. The paper had published a few stories in August, September and October 1973 on the company's troubles. The stories were brief, buried in the back pages. Evidently they had attracted little attention from the reporting and editing staffs.

Over a period of three months, the articles reported that the Securities and Exchange Commission had suspended over-the-counter trading in Home-Stake's common stock because of questions about the accuracy of its financial statements. The SEC had filed a suit accusing Home-Stake of fraud and had declared the company insolvent. Home-Stake and Robert Trippet, who had recently resigned as chairman, had sued each other. Trippet accused the new officers of mismanagement. They accused him of fraud. Home-Stake announced it would try to reorganize under the Bankruptcy Act. And Trippet agreed to an injunction against violations of federal securities law without admitting or denying that he had committed any violations.

Serious as such things may seem, they occur dozens of times a year in corporate America. The *Wall Street Journal* at least briefly acknowledges these actions when they involve one of the thousands of publicly owned companies whose stock prices are quoted in the paper. But unless the company is large, with many thousands of shareholders, or unless there is some other reason to believe that the situation is unusually significant, the paper normally will not launch a time-consuming investigation.

The Biggest Ponzi Scheme: A Reporter's Journal

On the surface, Home-Stake Production appeared to be one of the smallest companies the paper covered. Home-Stake had fewer than a thousand common stockholders and the total value of its common stock was less than $20 million. What the paper didn't know was that the most important and interesting investors in Home-Stake weren't its common stockholders; they were the mostly wealthy people, between two thousand and three thousand of them, who had invested more than $100 million in the "participation units" of Home-Stake's annual tax-sheltered oil drilling programs. This was far from apparent in what the *Journal* reported in the late summer and early fall of 1973. The suits and company announcements at that time never hinted at the prominence of Home-Stake's investors or the size of their investments.

Another, less important reason why the *Journal* failed to spot the Home-Stake story earlier was that it had no news bureau in Tulsa, where Home-Stake was headquartered. The nearest bureau was in Dallas.

On Friday, March 22, after reviewing our 1973 articles, I wrote a memorandum to John Barnett, the *Journal's* page-one editor, summarizing what I had learned and proposing that we look into the Home-Stake affair. He promptly agreed. I was still preoccupied that week with other work, but part of the following week was spent on the phone with several people outside New York to whom my friend Paul had referred me. I also spoke with a New York tax specialist who had helped me on previous stories and who, I correctly guessed, knew something about Home-Stake.

From them, I gleaned a few additional bits of information, mostly unconfirmed. Comedienne Phyllis Diller and several officers of General Electric Company were among the investors. The big Wall Street law firm of Simpson Thacher and Bartlett had passed upon parts of Home-Stake's offering circulars each year since the early 1960s. A number of accountants and lawyers had accepted payments from Home-Stake as inducements for encouraging their clients to invest in the drilling company, although nobody has accused anyone at Simpson Thacher and Bartlett of doing so.

The role of lawyers and accountants in the affair was interesting for two reasons.

First, the extent to which lawyers and accountants should be held partly responsible for illegal actions by their clients had become a controversial issue. The SEC, as well as private investors, had been trying with mixed results to attach part of the blame for violations of securities laws to the lawyers or accountants who advised the violators. And if Simpson Thacher and Bartlett had represented Home-Stake, it seemed to me that someone was almost certain to try to implicate the firm in the Home-Stake fraud.

Second, when a lawyer or accountant accepts money from a tax-shelter promoter as a reward for encouraging his client to invest money with the promoter, an obvious conflict of interest arises. The practice can be illegal. At a minimum, it tends to violate the ethical canons of the legal or accounting professions.

The people to whom I talked during the last week of March also told me that there was a massive amount of material on Home-Stake filed at the U.S. Court House in Tulsa in connection with the lawsuits that had been brought there. By that time I had accumulated a lot of hearsay, but very little documentary evidence usable in a story. So I decided to go to Tulsa and examine the court files. I arrived in Tulsa late on Tuesday, April 2. It was Academy Award night in Hollywood. Watching the last hour of the show on television in my hotel room, I wondered whether any of the stars who were receiving or presenting awards had invested in Home-Stake.

The next day I went to the clerk's office of the U. S. District Court and found well over a thousand pages of material on Home-Stake. There were files on the

SEC's civil suit, a bankruptcy trustee's investigation and several private lawsuits.

My first objective was to get a list of investors. Only with that could I determine once and for all how compelling the story was. If a few entertainers and General Electric executives, or a few thousand unknowns, had lost money, it would mean a brief story on the lure and peril of tax shelters and the apparent ingenuity of Home-Stake's scheme. If, on the other hand, the investors included a sizeable number of wealthy celebrities and corporate executives, and their losses amounted to anything approaching $100 million, it could prove to be one of the most spectacular swindles of all time. It would mean the fraud was so ingenious that it had duped, over a period of several years, a large cross-section of the most sophisticated financial minds in the nation, and a lot of others who could afford to hire the best investment and tax-planning advice available. This would set it apart from a typical stock manipulation that preys on less sophisticated victims.

A court clerk gave me a list of entries in the Home-Stake bankruptcy trustee's file. Any bankruptcy trustee's duties include fielding claims from investors; so it seemed logical that the roster of names I needed would be in the trustee's file. The file had been started in September 1973, when Home-Stake entered bankruptcy proceedings, and by the time of my visit in April, the list of entries covered several single-spaced typewritten pages. I scanned it and found that an investor list, containing names, addresses, and amounts of investment, was supposed to be a part of the record.

The clerk found the list buried in the back of a filing cabinet drawer. It was a mailing list, a computer printout of the names of people who supposedly owned Home-Stake drilling units as of November 1973. The list showed their addresses but not the amounts they had invested. I sat down at a table and started through it.

The first entry I recognized was Alan Alda, c/o International Business Management, 641 Lexington Avenue, New York City. (I already had Alda's name from Paul's list in New York.)

Then, interspersed with unfamiliar names, I came to:

—The American Cancer Society.

—Eaton Ballard, Broadway-Hale Stores, Los Angeles. (I knew Broadway-Hale was one of the biggest department-store chains on the West Coast, and I assumed Ballard was an executive.)

—Jack Benny, 444 UCB Building, 9601 Wilshire Boulevard, Beverly Hills, California (Probably the address of his accountant, lawyer or banker, I thought.)

—Candice Bergen, International Business Management, 641 Lexington Avenue, New York. (Same address as Alda; must be some sort of agency that handles the financial affairs of entertainers.)

—Professor Curtis Berger, Columbia University Law School, New York.

—Jacqueline Bisset, Suite 1132, 1901 Avenue of the Stars, Los Angeles. (I recognized the address as Century City and knew that a lot of show business lawyers and accountants had their offices there.)

—R. Burdell Bixby, 140 Broadway, New York. (Sounded like a Wall Street lawyer. The address fit. It's half a block from my office. The name rang a faint bell.)

—Bill Blass, 550 Seventh Avenue, New York. (The clothes designer.)

—Joseph Bologna and Renee Taylor Bologna, c/o Martin Melzer, 352 Seventh Avenue, New York. (I recognized them as the husband-and-wife screen-writing team who also pursue separate acting careers. In the past year I had seen two of their films, *Made For Each Other* and *Lovers and Other Strangers*.

—Martin Bregman; no address was given, but the name seemed familiar.

—Buffy Sainte-Marie Bugbee, 1900 Avenue of the

Stars, Los Angeles. (Under her maiden name, she is a well-known singer and song writer. Century City again. Probably another law or accounting firm.)

It was only necessary to go through the B's to conclude that there would be a lot of big names in entertainment, business and law. I began separate lists—entertainment–arts–writing, business–law, charities and a miscellaneous, for people who seemed familiar but whom I couldn't definitely place.

In the show business category I came to Diahann Carroll; David Cassidy; Jack Cassidy; Shirley Jones Cassidy; Oleg Cassini, the clothes designer; Philip D'Antoni, producer of the *French Connection*; Phyllis Diller; Robert (Bob) Dylan; Mia Farrow; George J. W. Goodman, who had written two best-selling books on money and finance under the pseudonym "Adam Smith;" Barbara Walters Guber, who, under her maiden name, helps preside over the "Today" television program.

In the business-law category I came across several immediately recognizable names: Thomas S. Gates of Morgan Guaranty Trust Company and Neil McElroy of Procter and Gamble, both former Secretaries of Defense. In most cases, rather than recognizing an investor's name, I recognized his business mailing address—a company like General Electric or a big Wall Street law firm like Sullivan and Cromwell. I suspected—and *Who's Who in America* would later confirm—that these people were the top officers or senior partners of the corporations or law firms where they got their Home-Stake mail. There were lots of General Electric names, as I had been told there would be.

It almost seemed a bonus that the list included three well-known politicians, Senators Jacob Javits of New York and Ernest Hollings of South Carolina and former Florida Governor Claude Kirk. No one had mentioned them before.

The charities were a blue-chip group, too. After the American Cancer Society came the American Jewish

Swindled!

Committee, Barnard College, Baylor University, the Boy Scouts, Brandeis, Columbia, Cornell, and Dartmouth Universities—and I had only gotten to the D's.

It took several hours to go over the more than two-thousand names. But by the end, the dimensions of the situation were clear. Instead of six or seven entertainers, I had the names of at least thirty show business celebrities, fifty-six prominent business executives and New York and Washington lawyers, thirty big charities, and about a dozen miscellaneous people I knew were notable for one reason or another. There were also dozens of unfamiliar names with high-rent addresses in Manhattan or Beverly Hills. And these names had been gleaned from a single rapid perusal of the list, without any research for further identification. (The roster of Home-Stake owners the *Journal* ultimately published contained the names of forty-five figures in arts and sports, fifty-one businessmen, twenty-seven lawyers and one hundred eleven charities, besides the three politicians.)

Because the list didn't say how much, when or under what circumstances people had invested, I had a long way to go. But the names alone warranted a major effort. Anyone or any company that could swindle people like these over an extended period certainly deserved a close look.

I decided to examine the other court files so I would be as knowledgeable as possible before interviewing anyone in Tulsa.

Voluminous as the files were, they failed to tell me how investors had been sold, or how much they had lost in Home-Stake. But the records did shed some new light on certain facets of the fraud and more important, they contained material that specifically documented some of the general allegations I had been hearing.

An affidavit in the SEC file, written by Sammy L. Hughes, a certified public accountant on the commission's investigative staff, presented a detailed analysis of Home-Stake's accounting and why it may have been fraudulent.

100

In particular, the affidavit gave details of a complex series of transactions whereby Home-Stake chairman Trippet allegedly had conspired with a New York tax lawyer, Kent M. Klineman, to funnel about $3 million out of Home-Stake.

The transcript of an SEC interrogation of Home-Stake's legal counsel, Tulsa lawyer Thomas A. Landrith Jr., indicated that Landrith had taken the Fifth Amendment when the questioning became substantive.

There were some specific references to lawyers' and accountants' having taken money in various ways from Home-Stake. David Melendy, Home-Stake's financial vice president, testified at a court hearing. According to him, the IRS had concluded that $42,000 paid to the New York accounting firm of Siegel and Goldburt amounted to a commission for selling Home-Stake investments to the firm's clients instead of a fee for accounting services. Who the clients were wasn't indicated.

A memorandum filed by the attorney for actor Walter Matthau alleged that Home-Stake had loaned a New York lawyer, William E. Murray, more than $150,000 and also made payments to a small company controlled by him. These facts hadn't been disclosed in Home-Stake's 1972 prospectus, for which Murray had written a supposedly objective tax opinion, the Matthau memorandum said.

I came across a copy of a claim the bankruptcy trustee had filed with the Aetna Casualty and Surety Company, attempting to collect on Home-Stake's insurance policy against fraud by company officers. The claim cited several instances where Robert Trippet allegedly had diverted money out of Home-Stake to phony corporations he controlled.

An Internal Revenue Service agent's report charged that out of the $23 million Home-Stake had raised in 1970 and promised to spend drilling for oil, only $3 million for drilling was actually spent.

Reading these documents and a lot of others, and copying much of the material on an IBM copier, consumed the rest of the week. On Thursday I cancelled a Friday flight I had booked back to New York and also cancelled a reservation for a New York Knicks playoff game at Madison Square Garden the following Tuesday.

By Saturday, I was drowning in detail. I decided to spend the weekend reviewing everything I had collected, organizing it, trying to absorb it and deciding where to go next. I thoroughly read or reread every document I had copied and every note I had taken since my session with Paul more than two weeks earlier. I noted each fact and allegation by category, in outline form on yellow legal-size sheets. I had a sheet for general facts about the company, one for personal details on Robert Trippet, one for the role of the lawyers and accountants, and so forth. I numbered each document and set of notes and keyed the outline to the numbers so I would know where to go to document any point.

Generally, the lawsuits contained similar allegations about the fraud, but in a few instances an accusation was made in only one suit. For example, several New York investors were the only ones to allege that Home-Stake had used sham oil wells at its California properties and had portrayed certain equipment as oil equipment when in fact it wasn't oil gear.

On Sunday I made a long list of questions to ask Robert Trippet, whom I anticipated trying to interview early in the coming week. In order to get a general impression of Trippet's life style, I looked up his address in the Tulsa phone directory and drove past his home that afternoon. It turned out to be a sprawling two-story white house, luxuriantly landscaped, in the most exclusive part of town.

My first appointment Monday, April 8, was with Richard Sonberg, the first Tulsa lawyer to bring a broad-based fraud suit against Trippet and Home-Stake. I had been told that investors had been suing or threatening to sue Trippet for years prior to the current rash of suits, but that he had managed to settle out of court.

Sonberg had filed suit on behalf of a group of New Yorkers in 1966, alleging some of the same fraudulent activities that the SEC and others would allege seven years later. These clients of Sonberg, including a justice of the New York State Supreme Court's appellate division, a Park Avenue physician, a lawyer and two businessmen, had begun buying Home-Stake drilling interests as far back as 1959.

They first complained to Trippet in 1962 about the low returns they were getting from their investments. The suit filed by Sonberg was settled in late 1967, when Trippet agreed to repay part of what the New Yorkers had invested. Sonberg said that he had reported his suit to the SEC at the time, but it had appeared disinterested.

At 11:15 that morning I went to see the Home-stake bankruptcy trustee, Royce H. Savage, at the Home-Stake offices on the tenth floor of Tulsa's ornate old Philtower Building. Savage, a kindly man of about seventy, had been a federal judge in Tulsa and general counsel of Gulf Oil Corporation. I told him the court files indicated that amounts people invested in Home-Stake, as well as their names and addresses, were supposed to be part of the record, but I had been able to find only the names and addresses. He called in David Melendy, the company's financial vice president, a nervous little man wearing a bow tie and smoking a cigarette. Savage told Melendy to give me whatever I needed.

Melendy and Don Richards, a Home-Stake CPA, showed me a computer printout list of people who owned Home-Stake shares as of November 23 1973. The list was somewhat similar to the one I had seen at the courthouse, but this list included the number of units of Home-Stake's annual drilling programs each investor had bought and the year of the purchases. Generally, that was enough to calculate the amount of the investments; I already knew what each year's units had been sold for.

But the list didn't include people who had disposed of their units before the effective date of the list. Jack Benny, for one, was missing, and I asked about him. Melendy left the room for a moment (apparently to look up Benny in a master file), and reported that Benny had invested $100,000 in 1969 and $200,000 in 1970, but later had sold three-fourths of his units back to Home-Stake and had contributed the others to the Jewish Federation Coucil of Greater Los Angeles.

Melendy had a secretary make a copy of the printout for me. I returned to my hotel room, went over it in detail and found that Jack Benny wasn't the only name that was missing. I was aided in this effort by a separate list of investors in the 1968 Home-Stake drilling program. I had obtained this list from a confidential source earlier, before I came to Tulsa. Walter B. Wriston, board chairman of New York's First National City Bank, the nation's second largest, was on record for a $40,000 investment in 1968. But he wasn't on the 1973 list. That meant he had disposed of his 1968 investment before November 23 1973. Whether he had invested in other years wasn't clear.

Comparing the 1973 list to the 1968 roster also gave me the beginning of an important insight into how several of the entertainers had gotten into Home-Stake. I noticed that the mailing address of several celebrities, Candice Bergen, for instance, was given as "Martin Bregman Inc." in 1968 and "International Business Management" in 1973. The companies had the same address, 641 Lexington Avenue, New York. I called New York City information and found that they also had the same phone number. The name "Martin Bregman" seemed familiar and I finally recalled that I had seen it at the courthouse on a list of people who had gotten loans from Home-Stake and hadn't paid them back on time. I tentatively surmised, and later confirmed, that Bregman was a financial manager for entertainers, that he had induced clients to invest in Home-Stake and that he had taken money from the company in the form of loans.

I phoned Trippet Tuesday morning and he invited me to come to his office at 2:00 P.M. Beforehand I stopped again at the Home-Stake office to ask a few more questions. David Melendy and Don Richards didn't seem as cordial as they had the day before. I asked for details on the year-to-year investments of Citibank's Walter Wriston. Melendy said they were sorry but they weren't able to give me any more information at that time.

I surmised that they had had second thoughts about the wisdom of being as open as they had been the day before. But I was still in the beginning stages of what would be a long investigation, and rather than antagonize important sources unnecessarily, I accepted their refusal for the time being.

When I arrived at Trippet's office, he had left word that I should be sent across the street to the office of his lawyer, James C. Lang. Lang is a former FBI agent and former assistant Tulsa County district attorney. The two men received me politely but diffidently. Trippet, looking older than his fifty-five years, was dressed in a blue pin-striped suit, white shirt and dark tie. He wore thick glasses and had a soft, deep speaking voice. Lang, a younger man, did most of the talking. After I explained what I wanted, Lang said that Trippet, as a lawyer himself, was prohibited by the legal profession's canons of ethics from commenting, outside the court record, on any charge then in litigation. That included just about everything on my list. All Trippet would do was confirm his age, address and educational background. Counting idle chit-chat, the interview lasted about ten minutes.

During these early stages of reporting, I also talked in person or by phone with several lawyers for groups of investors who had filed suit against the drilling concern. The attorneys included R. Dobie Langenkamp of the Tulsa firm of Doerner, Stuart, Saunders, Daniel and Langenkamp;

Peter Van N. Lockwood of Caplin and Drysdale in Washington, D.C., and William A. Wineberg Jr. of the San Francisco firm of Broad, Khourie and Schulz. I talked with the bankruptcy trustee's two lawyers, A. F. Ringold and Gene L. Mortensen of the Tulsa firm of Rosenstein, Fist and Ringold. I talked with Cecil S. Mathis, chief enforcement attorney of the SEC's regional office in Fort Worth. And I talked with Stephen V. Wilson, chief of the fraud and special prosecutions unit of the U.S. attorney's office in Los Angeles. Mathis had headed the team of investigators that brought the SEC's fraud suit against Home-Stake. Wilson was to head the Justice Department's investigation of the case and present it to a federal grand jury.

All of these lawyers were as helpful as they could be within the restrictions imposed by legal ethics and government rules on the disclosure of information about pending cases that isn't part of the public court record.

After a few more trips to the courthouse and the IBM copier, I was overwhelmed again with facts to be sorted out. Had other newspapers known about the Home-Stake swindle and been competing to publish the story first, I could have written mine on the spot. It would have contained most of the big names, an authoritative outline of the alleged swindle and an estimate of the amount of money involved. But I could have given only a general and speculative answer to the most intriguing question: How did all these wealthy, sophisticated people happen to invest in this particular tax shelter? So far as I knew (and I had arranged to be warned) no other papers were yet aware of the story. I chose to return to New York and pursue the "how" question, a task I knew would be time-consuming but essential.

I arrived back at my office on the morning of Thursday, April 11. After handling another story, unrelated to Home-Stake, I briefed the *Journal* editors and set about the mundane chore of getting the mass of material I had collected into a form I could use efficiently. I made a second copy of the investor list for safe-keeping and installed the primary copy—324 pages—in a loose-leaf binder. I extracted the names of about one hundred more or less prominent people whom I wanted to contact and put each name and the amount of his or her investment at the top of a separate blank sheet. Those sheets I inserted alphabetically in the front of the binder.

For almost all of the next four weeks, I telephoned and talked in person to dozens of businessmen and lawyers in the New York City area who had invested in Home-Stake and thus had been in direct contact with either Trippet or other Home-Stake officials. I postponed calling show-business people since they have a lot of contact with the press, and I feared other journalists would get tipped off.

I began with the least prominent of the businessmen and lawyers, people from whom I was willing to accept information in exchange for not naming them. I couldn't make that kind of deal with the famous executives and attorneys; it was their names that helped make the story interesting. As it turned out, a surprisingly large number of both the famous and less famous were willing to talk on the record.

From these conversations I was able to build a solid picture of the informal but highly potent network of word-of-mouth contacts Home-Stake had established in New York over the years. Corporate executives, bankers and lawyers were influenced more by their peers in the business world than by conventional sources of advice such as investment analysts and stockbrokers. Hoyt Ammidon, chairman of the board of New York's U.S. Trust, told me: "Our oil investment experts were against Home-Stake from the beginning, but I knew several top people at GE and First National City Bank had invested. Because these two organizations, including the head of the oil department at City, liked it, it seemed to me to have merit."

Many of these men had met Robert Trippet personally. Several of them also confirmed the key role that New York tax lawyer William E. Murray had played in selling

Home-Stake. (Murray, the Tulsa court files revealed, had been lent more than $150,000 by Home-Stake.) Murray's name was mentioned by Hoyt Ammidon; Dean Fite, vice president and group executive of Procter and Gamble; Chester Nimitz Jr., chairman of a Connecticut scientific-instruments company and son of the late World War II admiral; and Robert J. McDonald, a senior partner at Sullivan and Cromwell, the New York law firm.

William Morton, a brusque former president of American Express Company, told me that he first heard of Home-Stake when he walked into the locker room of his country club one Sunday morning. "I ran into two friends of mine," he said. "One of them heads one of the biggest banks in the world. They said, 'Bill, you should be in this.' I said 'What is it?' They told me about Home-Stake. I said, 'Send him (Trippet) around to see me.' I guess I'm stupid and just don't understand oil people. I went along. He (Trippet) is the biggest flim flam man ever to hit Wall Street. Later I was encouraged to give it to charity, but I didn't believe it was worth what they said. Thank God I didn't give mine to the Museum of Modern Art or Dartmouth."

After that, Morton said: "By the way, this is all off the record." I politely explained that a call from a journalist is on the record unless otherwise specified at the outset. He accused me of not having any integrity.

Most of the General Electric officers who had invested in Home-Stake refused to take my calls. The most interesting GE figure was the company's former chairman, Fred J. Borch, an internationally famous executive. Borch invested $440,920 in Home-Stake. He had recently retired and no one at the company would give me his phone number. I learned that he had homes in Naples, Florida, and New Canaan, Connecticut. The Florida number had been disconnected. The Connecticut number was unlisted. Finally I looked up Borch in *Who's Who in America* and phoned each of his private clubs listed there. An attendant at one gave me his Connecticut phone number. I dialed it and Borch answered. His first words, after I identified myself and gave my reason for calling, were: "How did you get my number?"

I said a mutual acquaintance had given it to me. He said he had nothing to say and hung up.

I had no more success with the lawyer who represented the General Electric officers in their suits against Home-Stake. I had known him before when he was an assistant U.S. attorney in Manhattan investigating the fraudulent activities of a company called National Student Marketing Corporation. I had covered NSMC's spectacular collapse in the stock market for the *Journal* in 1970. The lawyer had filed several suits in Tulsa since my visit there in early April, and I asked for copies of them. Although they were on the public record in Tulsa, it was much more convenient for me to study them in New York. The lawyer agreed and told me to send a messenger uptown to his office.

When the messenger arrived, the lawyer had disappeared and a secretary told the messenger that she couldn't give him the material. The attorney later phoned me to say his clients had refused to let him cooperate with me in any way, even by giving me copies of public documents.

In researching the show-business figures' investments in Home-Stake, my first objective was to explore the role of Martin Bregman. His business-management agency at 641 Lexington Avenue was or had been the business mailing address of a number of luminaries, including Liza Minnelli, Barbra Streisand, Alan Alda, Barbara Walters, Sandy Dennis, Candice Bergen, Bill Blass, Joseph Bologna, Renee Taylor, Oleg Cassini and Faye Dunaway. The court records in Tulsa showed that Bregman had taken money from Home-Stake in the form of loans.

I had heard that Bregman had been put in touch with Home-Stake by New York tax lawyer Kent Klineman, who also had taken money from Home-Stake and appeared to have helped Robert Trippet divert about $3 million out of the company. I phoned several people who knew Bregman or Klineman or both and got some background information on them. But I still wasn't able to confirm that Klineman was the link. Surprisingly, Martin Bregman confirmed that himself the first time I called him. He said he had met Trippet through a "lawyer, a mutual friend." "That was Kent Klineman, wasn't it," I ventured. "Yes," Bregman replied. Bregman also confirmed that he represented the entertainers whose Home-Stake mail went to his address. He refused to say more at that point, but the brief talk was a breakthrough. It confirmed how a sizeable number of celebrities had happened to invest in Home-Stake.

My first contact with Kent Klineman was much less productive. He wouldn't tell me anything.

In early May I phoned David Melendy, the Home-Stake financial vice president in Tulsa, to see if he would part with some of the information on individual investors he had refused to divulge a few weeks earlier. Melendy was on vacation, but Don Richards, the accountant who had witnessed all my conversations with Melendy, readily agreed to help. He gave me the year-by-year investments of Walter Wriston, the Citibank chairman; George Moore, the immediate past Citibank chairman; former GE head Fred Borch, and one Howard A. Williams, who I had decided might be singer Andy Williams. Richards also told me the names of charities to which these men had given some of their Home-Stake shares. I felt no obligation to remind Richards that he and Melendy had been reluctant to give me this information three weeks earlier.

By the second week in May, I had gathered enough material on Home-Stake's New York operations and prepared to leave for Los Angeles. Home-Stake had mounted nearly as large a sales effort there as it had in New York, and its principal oil-drilling properties in the 1960s were near Santa Maria, California, a small community just north of Santa Barbara. It was at those properties that Home-Stake had allegedly painted a farmer's irrigation piping so it

110

would appear to be part of the company's oil production network.

Before going to California, I phoned Harry L. Fitzgerald, who had been one of Home-Stake's top sales vice presidents. Most former company officers had refused to talk to me, but the Fitzgerald interview was another breakthrough. He had organized the Los Angeles sales force in the early 1960s, and now he outlined the key people in it. Robert Trippet had sent Fitzgerald to Trippet's cousin, Oscar, a prominent Los Angeles lawyer. Oscar Trippet referred Fitzgerald to Donald McKee, a wealthy investment banker and business consultant. And McKee referred him to, among others, a Beverly Hills law firm which Fitzgerald told me was called Meyer Rosenfeld and Susman. The firm's clients, he said, included Jack Benny, Andy Williams and other entertainers.

Los Angeles information hadn't any listing for Meyer Rosenfeld and Susman, but the operator finally came up with Rosenfeld, Meyer and Susman, 9601 Wilshire Boulevard. I recalled that was the building where Jack Benny got his Home-Stake mail. I skimmed through the investor list and discovered that Ed Ames, Brenda Vacarro, Bobbie Gentry, Howard A. Williams and several people I hadn't heard of also got their mail there.

Also before leaving New York, I got the name and address in California of a petroleum engineer who had worked at Home-Stake's California oil drilling installation and had first-hand knowledge of the pipe-painting episode.

I flew to Los Angeles the evening of Monday, May 13, checked into the Beverly Wilshire Hotel and for the next two days interviewed several people in Beverly Hills and elsewhere in Southern California who had invested in Home-Stake.

Reliable sources explained in detail how Donald McKee had been contacted by Oscar Trippet and had referred Harry Fitzgerald to others, including the law firm of Rosenfeld, Meyer and Susman. It turned out that Martin Bregman, the New York agent, had put Home-Stake in touch with several people in California as well as those in New York.

A prominent certified public accountant, Ralph Jones, told me how the GE and Citibank officers' names had been dropped by Home-Stake salesmen in Los Angeles just as they had been in New York. John Guedel, producer of the old Art Linkletter "House Party" and "People Are Funny" shows and a client of Ralph Jones, said how impressed he had been with the apparent conservatism of the Home-Stake sales approach. "This didn't appear to be a suede-shoe thing. Ralph Jones is the most conservative man I ever met," Guedel said.

I hadn't had much luck in contacting the celebrities directly. So in New York I had gone to an agency called Celebrity Service that sells their telephone numbers for five dollars each. I bought Jack Benny, Buddy Hackett, Liza Minnelli, Jack Cassidy, Shirley Jones, Walter Matthau, James Coburn, Ozzie Nelson and Andy Williams.

Andy Williams' secretary refused to put me through to Williams but at least confirmed he was the Howard A. Williams on the Home-Stake investor list.

Then I dialed Buddy Hackett's number. An answering-service operator put me through and the unmistakable voice of Buddy Hackett came on the line.

"Mr. Hackett?"

"Yeah."

"This is David McClintick of the *Wall Street Journal* calling. Sorry to bother you at home. I'm doing some research on a company in which you have a rather sizeable investment. It's an oil-drilling outfit in Oklahoma called Home-Stake Production Company that has run into some financial difficulty. I'm not singling you out. I've talked to dozens of other investors, just trying to get some insight into how people got into this. And I wondered if you could tell me how you happened to make your investment.

"I haven't the vaguest idea."

"You've never heard of Home-Stake?"

"No, I just tell jokes. My accountant would handle that. How much do I have in it?"

"$208,000."

"I can't believe I would be in anything like that."

"Your accountant is Wallace Sheft, isn't he?" (The investor list indicated Hackett got his Home-Stake mail in care of Wallace Sheft, a New York CPA.)

"Yeah."

"Do you suppose he would know how this investment happened to be made?"

"I'm sure he would. My lawyer and accountant look into these things and explain them to me in baby talk. If it sounds okay, we go ahead."

"Maybe I'd better contact Mr. Sheft then."

"Yeah, he'd know about it. I'll tell you what I do know about."

"What's that?"

"Antique guns. That's what I invest in mostly."

"So you would recommend antique guns as an investment?"

"Yeah."

"Okay. Again, sorry to have bothered you. Thanks very much."

A call to the Jack Cassidy-Shirley Jones residence in Beverly Hills led to the Fairmont Hotel in Dallas, where they had just opened a new night club act. I waited until noon, Dallas time, to call, but still woke Cassidy from a sound sleep. He was as pleasant as he could be under the circumstances, but didn't have much to say and asked me to call back later. The second call elicited a referral to his accountant in Los Angeles, Leon Bush. Bush refused to talk, but my investor list revealed that Bush personally had a large investment in Home-Stake. I found later that his brother-in-law, a wealthy businessman and Home-Stake investor who maintains homes in Connecticut and Palm Springs, California, had recommended it to him. The total

Cassidy-Jones investment, including that of Jack's son, rock singer David Cassidy, was $300,000.

I conducted most of my interviews with Home-Stake investors by phone. Over the years I've found that people who have a small amount of valuable information but are likely to be reluctant to talk are more likely to say something useful if I phone them without warning, begin the conversation gently by apologizing for bothering them, then try to ease them into talking about the subject. If a journalist calls and sets up an appointment to see them in person, they frequently will have second thoughts and a secretary will call later and say the interview is off. In many other situations, however, face-to-face interviews are preferable—if publicity won't embarrass the person being interviewed, if he has nothing to lose by talking, if there's no need to quote him by name, or if he is so central to the story that failure to see him in person would leave an unacceptable gap in the article.

For a change of pace from the Beverly Hills set, I phoned Harvey Garland, the former Home-Stake engineer whose name and address I had obtained before leaving New York. Garland had quit Home-Stake in 1971, left the oil business and moved to Las Vegas. He took an accounting and tax-return preparation course and then bought the H. & R. Block franchise in Twenty Nine Palms, California, a small desert community three hours by car east of Los Angeles. Garland agreed to see me at 3:00 P.M. the next day, Thursday, May 16.

When I got to Twenty Nine Palms it was windy and dusty, and the temperature was in the nineties. Garland's tax-preparation office is in the front of a one-story building; he and his wife live in the back. We talked in his office. Garland is a large, chunky man in his late forties. He chain-smoked filter cigarettes and seemed nervous at first, but generally he was cooperative and gave direct answers to my questions. He had already been grilled by SEC investigators and two pairs of lawyers from Tulsa.

For two and a half hours (the last hour over cocktails served by his wife), Garland regaled me with tales of what it was like to work in Santa Maria for Home-Stake and Robert Trippet; how the local Home-Stake workers had considered the pipe-painting episode ridiculous, but Home-Stake officials had insisted on it; how Home-Stake had recorded certain five-hundred-foot holes it drilled as oil wells when it knew there wasn't any oil at five hundred feet; how the Santa Maria staff had put on a somewhat misleading show for wealthy investors, including actor Elliott Gould and GE's Fred Borch, who had flown in to inspect the drilling operations.

"Don't ask me where the money went, because I don't know," Garland said.

I drove back to Los Angeles that evening. The next day, Friday, I talked to several people without much success. Liza Minnelli's secretary, Diana Wemple, was pleasant, but said she knew Liza wouldn't talk except through her lawyer or accountant. Her lawyer is Mickey Rudin—he also represents Frank Sinatra—and he has a policy of never taking a phone call from a journalist inquiring about one of his clients. Liza's accountant, Sonny Golden, was hostile and uncooperative.

Don Rosenfeld, the senior partner in Rosenfeld, Meyer and Susman, refused to talk. I wasn't able to reach Jack Benny.

I phoned David Melendy, the Home-Stake financial vice president in Tulsa, to try to get a few more tidbits of information on some of the investors. Melendy angrily accused me of using deceit and trickery in extracting information from Don Richards over the phone two weeks previously. Melendy said he would have no more to say to me and hung up.

That evening the world premiere of the movie *That's Entertainment* was held at the Beverly Theater across the street from the Beverly Wilshire. The premiere was followed by a gala reception in the hotel ballroom. There were lots of stars around all day, but unfortunately, those I could get close to had nothing to do with Home-Stake.

I went out to dinner with friends from the Los Angeles bureau of the *Journal*. We were to be joined by a *Los Angeles Times* reporter and his wife. I was getting paranoid about possible competition from other papers on the Home-Stake story; so, totally unnecessarily, I warned the *Journal* people against letting anything slip to the *Times* reporter.

While waiting in the bar of the restaurant for a table, we watched the live television reports of the Los Angeles police confrontation with the Symbionese Liberation Army in their hideout. As they exchanged gunfire and the hideout burned, killing all six of the SLA members within, I reflected on my week spent in the midst of Beverly Hills opulence, desert heat and dust, and fraud, greed and tax-chiseling on Wilshire Boulevard and the Avenue of the Stars.

I couldn't help recalling a little of the Los Angeles of Nathaniel West and Joan Didion. No doubt, the bourbon I had consumed by that point in the evening inflated these literary musings.

Because of my fruitful interview with Harvey Garland and informative chats with other people who had witnessed Home-Stake's activities in Santa Maria, California, I decided not to take the time to visit the Santa Maria installation on this California trip. I flew to Tulsa on Sunday and spent the first part of the week filling some gaps in my information from the court records and talking to a few people I had missed on my first trip in April.

Back in New York Thursday, May 23, I was worrying anew about competition from other publications. I had been tipped that a business periodical published in Dallas and circulated throughout the Southwest was preparing an article on the Home-Stake swindle. I had visions of an Associated Press editor's seeing it and putting out the story across the country. The story wouldn't have been nearly as thorough as ours, but it would have skimmed off the cream and soured the heady pleasure of breaking a big story.

The writing of my story, which I had outlined in some detail by then, went fairly rapidly. Actually I wrote two stories. To avoid diluting their impact, they ultimately were combined into one. However, the most time-consuming task in late May and early June wasn't writing. It was compiling an accurate list of the famous investors, their current and past job titles or other identifying details and the amounts of their investments. The *Journal* was planning to publish the list along with the article.

There were 126 names, nearly that many dollar figures, and a comparable number of job titles and other details. The dollar amounts had to be derived by multiplying the number of drilling units an investor had bought in a particular year by the price each unit sold for (differing amounts in different years) and then adding the annual amounts together. Each fact and figure had to be checked and double-checked.

Some of the corporate executives had changed jobs once or twice since they invested in Home-Stake. I spent many hours with *Who's Who in America, Who's Who in Commerce and Industry* and corporate annual reports for the past ten years. Virgil Day, who had been a General Electric vice president when he began investing, was named by President Nixon to the Price Commission during the wage-price control period and then had moved to a New York law firm.

Who's Who also helped with some of the less familiar names. Michael Sovern turned out to be dean of the Columbia University law school. Leopold Godowsky, the concert violinist, also turned out to be the co-inventor of Kodachrome film processing and husband of the former Frances Gershwin. I phoned Godowsky to ask about his investment, and in the process confirmed that Frances Gershwin was the late George Gershwin's sister.

Another useful tool was the *Martindale-Hubbell Law*

117

Directory. I noted the names of the seventeen partners of Rosenfeld, Meyer and Susman in Beverly Hills and found ten of them on the Home-Stake investor list. I also got one of them to explain to me over the phone, in a form I could use without attributing it to him, how they happened to invest and how their and their clients' investments had been financed.

I had saved several interviews for the last minute. One was with George J. W. Goodman, the author, under the pseudonym "Adam Smith," of *The Money Game* and *Supermoney.* He also writes for *New York Magazine*; I was afraid that if I had called him sooner, he might have tried to write the Home-Stake story himself and break it in the magazine. (He had written in the past about his personal experiences with investment. The last time I had talked to him was just after he lost $50,000 in the collapse of the Basel, Switzerland, branch of the United California Bank.)

Actually, the main reason I called Goodman in connection with Home-Stake was to check a story I had heard from two witnesses that he had been sold his $110,000 Home-Stake investment over lunch at the Harvard Club of New York. He denied that, and accused me of dwelling on trivial details at the expense of the overall significance of the story. I assured him my research into the broad themes had been more than thorough and said I was sure that he, as a writer of colorful prose, could appreciate my desire to include pointed details in my article and make sure they were accurate. That didn't melt his hostility, and the interview amounted to little.

I turned in the last part of my story on Monday, June 10 1974. It was given to Donald Moffitt, page-one editor who frequently handles major investigative stories involving complex financial manipulations. Moffitt asked me several questions about the story and requested that some points be bolstered with additional detail. One of his concerns was that the article didn't give a precise enough estimate of the investors' losses. I had written that Home-Stake was

118

believed to have collected more than $100 million and returned only a small fraction of that. I didn't feel we could, with certainty, be any more specific.

However, I spent three more days on the company's records, pulling together figures from financial statements, court affidavits and other documents. After hundreds of adding-machine calculations, I concluded Home-Stake had taken in roughly $130 million and repaid possibly no more than $30 million, for a net pre-tax loss of $100 million. Of course, as the initial story explained, investors were able to cut that loss by taking tax deductions.

Another last-minute task was gathering some additional detail on Charles Ponzi, the late Boston swindler for whom Ponzi schemes are named. I had looked up a Supreme Court case, mentioned in one of the Home-Stake court files, which described how and when Ponzi had operated. But the case didn't say anything about his fate. Moffitt recalled that the *New Yorker* had published something on Ponzi many years ago. I got a copy of the article and it gave us the details we needed.

Charles Ponzi was a small, dapper Italian immigrant who, in 1919 at the age of thirty-seven, thought he had discovered a way to get rich. His scheme involved so-called "international reply coupons," which were designed to be included with letters sent abroad as prepayment for posting a reply. The price of the coupons was fixed in each country and didn't change as currency values fluctuated.

European currencies were depressed at the time, relative to the U.S. dollar, and Ponzi's idea was to send U.S. currency to confederates in Europe, have them convert it into their currencies, buy international reply coupons and send them to him. He then would redeem them in U.S. stamps worth more, because of the higher relative value of the dollar, than the money he had sent overseas. Theoretically the profit could exceed 200 percent.

Ponzi offered to pay an investor $1.50 in forty-five days

for every dollar invested. Word spread fast. The crowds of investors outside Ponzi's Boston office grew so large they blocked traffic. Ponzi found it was far easier to pay off early investors with later investors' contributions than to grapple with the cumbersome mechanics of the coupon exchange, whose feasibility was questionable anyway.

Ponzi took in more than $10 million before the scheme collapsed after several months under the weight of bad publicity and official investigations. He went to prison for fraud.

The *Wall Street Journal* published its first Home-Stake story on page one on Wednesday, June 26 1974. The final stages of preparation absorbed me so much that I didn't give a thought until that morning to how the story might be followed up with others, exploring certain aspects of the swindle in more detail. I dashed off a memo proposing three additional pieces. The following Monday morning, July 1, I took TWA Flight 73 back to Tulsa.

My first stop in Tulsa was the federal court house. Since I last was there on May 22, some important new material had accumulated. A group of about 120 investors, including Fred Borch, Russell McFall and other present and past General Electric and Western Union executives, had filed precise accountings of their Home-Stake losses from 1964 through 1972.

I stayed up past midnight analyzing the figures. The next morning, I dictated a story to the New York office of the *Journal*. The story said the group of 120 investors claimed a total loss of $8.8 million, or 81 percent of the $10.9 million they had entrusted to Home-Stake.

On Wednesday, July 3, I called on Royce Savage, Home-Stake's court-appointed bankruptcy trustee. I wanted to get to know him better. I also thought he could help repair my shattered relations with David Melendy, the Home-Stake financial vice president who in May had accused me of deceit and trickery in extracting information from the company accountant, Don Richards. Melendy's cooperation was essential if I were to write a story telling what Home-Stake and Robert Trippet had done with all the money they had collected and hadn't spent drilling for oil.

Savage greeted me cordially. If he ever had been angry that Richards had given me information—as Melendy said Savage had been—he didn't show it. He accepted my explanation that there had been an innocent misunderstanding. He promised to see that Melendy gave me full cooperation. I took the late afternoon flight back to New York to relax over the four-day July 4 weekend.

(Editor's note: By the week of July 4, McClintick's first Home-Stake story had caught the attention of the nation and, indeed, much of the rest of the world. It was a major story on network news broadcasts; front-page material for such newspapers as the *New York Times, New York Post* and *Washington Post* and the subject of articles in *Time, Newsweek* and Britain's *Financial Times.*)

The next Monday found me back in Tulsa to begin a frustrating and barely productive two weeks. I made little progress in tracing the missing $100 million. I got bogged down in trivial aspects of the alleged swindle. Shuttling constantly between air-conditioned buildings and Tulsa's 100-degree summer heat, I caught a severe cold.

Still, Melendy's hostility was melting, if slowly. In submerging myself in the records—Home-Stake's yearly financial statements, prospectuses and other documents—I found some clues to the disposition of some of the missing money. And I got better acquainted with several Tulsans who later would prove helpful.

At midnight on Friday, July 12, I was sipping lemonade with some prominent citizens by a swimming pool at the home of a lawyer who wasn't involved with Home-Stake. From some of the guests I heard several intriguing anecdotes about the early career of Robert Trippet. The tales suggested that the roots of the Home-Stake affair might lie deeper than I had thought.

121

Swindled!

Eventually I learned that, even as early as his college days, Trippet had been considered "overbearing." A woman who dated him said he was "cocky," and a section of his University of Oklahoma yearbook described him as having a "big car, big money, and a big mouth." As a lawyer, he quickly earned a reputation for pressing for every advantage in a deal, more out of a desire to exercise his own superiority than out of professional duty. And although Robert Trippet came from an old and wealthy Oklahoma family, he once went to extraordinary lengths to avoid paying taxes on the cigarettes he purchased out-of-state by mail. In fact, it wasn't until he was threatened with loss of part of his property that he grudgingly agreed to make restitution for the past-due Oklahoma state taxes.

My editors didn't want a profile of Trippet until later. So I wrote a story on what Home-Stake and Trippet had done with the missing money. The story didn't fully answer the question. It told, roughly, how much Trippet was accused of having taken, how much the company had spent drilling for oil and how much it had poured into its costly sales effort. But there were still many millions of dollars unaccounted for. (More than a year later, auditors still were unable to account for several million.)

There were other stories to be written; Home-Stake had practically become my career. In September, I began looking into why the alleged swindle hadn't collapsed years before it did. When investors complained of lower-than-promised returns, Home-Stake typically had recommended that they donate their shares to charity and take another tax deduction. Home-Stake provided geological analyses, purportedly disinterested, that placed a high value on the shares. An investor could show the appraisal to the Internal Revenue Service if it challenged the value of his deduction. Instead of suing Home-Stake, many high-bracket investors chose to cut their losses by giving away their shares.

The charities that got them were much less willing to

122

talk about their Home-Stake holdings than the original investors had been. The charities were reluctant to offend their benefactors, many of whom had contributed, over the years, hard cash and valuable securities.

To this taciturnity there were exceptions. The U.S. Library of Congress unhesitatingly disclosed that it got a sizable block of Home-Stake shares from Martin Bregman and several of his clients. Bregman was the New York movie producer and manager of entertainers' money, and the donors included Candice Bergen and Alan Alda. The gifts came late in 1971 and late in 1972. That was after the SEC filed its initial suit, signaling that all wasn't well with Home-Stake.

More difficult to determine was the manner in which something called Dartmouth Realty and Oil Corporation, c/o Wilson W. Curtis, Vice President and Trust Officer, Durfee Trust Company, Fall River, Massachusetts, wound up holding a large block of Home-Stake shares. At first I assumed that Dartmouth Realty and Oil had been created to receive certain gifts to Dartmouth College, but Dartmouth College's financial officer told me it wasn't so.

When I tried to reach Wilson Curtis, I was told he had retired. His successor at the trust company never had heard of Dartmouth Realty and Oil. I reached the retired Curtis at home, and he explained that the corporation had been created to receive gifts for the Southeastern Massachusetts University Educational Foundation. The university is located in North Dartmouth, Massachusetts. I flew to North Dartmouth aboard an old Air New England DC-3. There I learned that William E. Murray had helped create the foundation. Murray figured prominently as a defendant in several fraud suits against Home-Stake. The foundation had given little money to the university, because the foundation's assets consisted almost entirely of shares in Home-Stake. The shares had come as tax-deductible contributions from clients of Murray, a tax lawyer.

In October, I went to California again to report how

Swindled!

Home-Stake had dressed up its "oil field" at Santa Maria. An ex-employee showed me around. He pointed out the farmer's irrigation pipes that Home-Stake had painted pink and orange to look like oil piping. The paint had weathered, but enough remained to make it easy to picture how the pipes looked five years before.

A federal grand jury in Los Angeles was investigating the Home-Stake affair, and only few ex-employees would talk with me without my assurance that I wouldn't print their names. Gene Bonetto, an ex-roustabout for Home-Stake, was one who did talk. I ran into Gene in Santa Maria, and we had hamburgers and coffee at Pappy's Truck Stop, just outside town. Gene said he and other employees had called the Santa Maria field "the funny farm." Why? "No normal oil company," Gene said, "would operate the way Home-Stake did."

Back again in California in December, I reported the indictment of the men who allegedly took part in the fraud. Trippet and twelve others were charged with forty-five counts of conspiracy, tax fraud, securities fraud and mail fraud. One minor defendant pleaded guilty. By early 1976, criminal charges against three men, including Tulsa lawyer Thomas Landrith, had been dropped, and Trippet and the other eight were awaiting trial. The complexity of the case, and the burden it would place on the federal courts, had delayed the trial. Some 29 lawsuits against Home-Stake also were moving slowly.

While still in California, I researched yet another story growing out of Home-Stake: how it was that many show-business folk had been exploited by unscrupulous financial managers and advisors. At the time, Doris Day had just won a court judgment for $23 million against her former lawyer for having allegedly mismanaged her money over a period of eighteen years.

Though I spent days reading the voluminous record in the case, I wanted to interview Doris Day in person. I could already see her in the lead of the story. She would be

lounging on her sun-drenched poolside patio in Beverly
Hills, sipping a glass of milk and quietly stroking the neck
of one of her eleven dogs. She would appear the very picture of contentment and financial security. But wait, dear
reader! This is a not-so-rich superstar. Her lawyer has
squandered her money.

That, very roughly, was what I had hoped for. Miss Day's
new lawyer did assure me that I could see her. But as the
days passed it became apparent that either my timing was
poor or Doris Day simply didn't want to talk. First, I was
told she was exhausted from having taped a television special with John Denver. Then she got a virus. And then I
was told two of those eleven dogs got into a fight. When she
tried to break it up, one of them bit her. That sent her to a
hospital emergency room for treatment, and she couldn't
see me for a while longer.

When you're a newspaper writer, and your lead falls
through, you are frustrated.

So, frustrated, I boarded a TWA flight back to New York
on Wednesday, December 18. As I settled into a seat in the
first-class cabin, I heard a familiar British accent. In front of
me was Julie Andrews. I looked across the aisle. There was
Kevin McCarthy. And right behind him was a famous
female entertainer whom I have promised anonymity.
Let's call her Sara Star.

As I sipped a cocktail, it occurred to me that if any of
these entertainers had money problems with their lawyers
or accountants, I would have a lead for my story.

Braced with a Bloody Mary, I struck up a conversation
with Sara Star. I told her who I was and what I wanted. She
had serious trouble with her accountant, she said; he had
stolen money from her. I tried not to appear elated. She
asked me not to identify her in my story because she probably would sue the accountant, and she didn't want to tip
her hand. But she invited me to sit down and hear the
whole tale. She even asked me to recommend a reliable
accountant in New York.

Swindled!

By the time Sara Star had told all, Kevin McCarthy was asleep. When Julie Andrews' seatmate went to the lavatory, I moved in, apologizing for intruding. Among other things, I told her that I had seen her in *My Fair Lady* at the Mark Hellinger Theater in New York in July 1957 and in *Camelot* at the Colonial Theater in Boston in November 1960. Then I explained what I was doing. Miss Andrews said she hadn't any problems with money managers, but she knew many other entertainers who have had. Then she uttered the memorable quote I needed to finish off my story, which appeared in the *Journal* March 21 1975. Summing up the fears of the many prominent people who had invested in or heard about Home-Stake, Julie Andrews said:

"It makes you wonder whether you shouldn't put all you have into a nice Van Gogh painting, so you can hang it on the wall and say, 'There. It's all there.'"

V

"Necessary" Payoffs—
But Who Really Pays?

By Jonathan Kwitny

"Currier Holman will never get hurt, because he always hits the other fellow twice as hard as the other fellow hits him."
—Knute Rockne of Notre Dame,
as quoted by Currier Holman's brother, Grant.

It is 1970, and the two men who may be the most powerful in the American meat industry have come face to face. Other than power, they seem to have little in common.

Currier J. Holman is the tall, graying, even-featured tintype of the Midwestern business success that he is. His adversary, Moe Steinman, is a mean little manipulator, gruff and inarticulate.

It has been less than ten years since Holman, a veteran cattleman, founded Iowa Beef Processors Inc., a company based on a vision he had been developing for a quarter of a century. In all that time he had watched packing plants ship whole, swinging carcasses of beef around the country.

Although they had always done so, Holman sensed that butchering the beef at the slaughterpoint and shipping it in boxes would result in enormous economies. Now, in less than a decade of actively pursuing that idea, he has built Iowa Beef into the largest meat processing firm in the world. His company, and others that borrowed from its innovations, have swept past the inefficient old giants of the industry, Swift and Armour. Holman and a few associates have revolutionized the way beef in the United States is slaughtered and transported, as probably no other American industry has been revolutionized since the days of Henry Ford. Iowa Beef's innovations can potentially save consumers many cents a pound on the meat they buy.

Now, Currier Holman is confronting the one obstacle left in the way of his dream. That obstacle is the traditional method by which the beef, after being slaughtered and transported, is distributed to the public. Unlike the processing system that Holman has transformed, the distribution system is not so much inept as it is corrupt. It wipes out the savings from Iowa Beef's processing innovations and then some. And it is so firmly entrenched that against it, Currier Holman's revolution seems about to collapse.

While Currier Holman was the product of private military academies and Notre Dame, Moe Steinman was a child immigrant from Poland with no formal education. While Currier Holman was sweating out his young manhood gutting carcasses in Sioux City slaughterhouses, carefully noting every inefficiency he could find, Moe Steinman was forming lifelong relationships with Mafia racketeers on the streets of the Bronx. While Currier Holman was building the biggest balance sheet in the beef industry, Moe Steinman was cementing his position as the one middleman you had to hire if you wanted supermarket chain executives to buy your meat or union butchers to handle it in or near the world's largest meat market, New York City.

Now they seem to be avoiding each other's glances. It is Steinman's turf, his favorite negotiating place, a room at a Manhattan hotel, the Stanhope. Holman will recall later that "the blinds were closed . . . it was very dark and difficult to see. . . ." Holman is accompanied by his partner in founding Iowa Beef, A. D. (Andy) Anderson, and by their corporate counsel, P. L. Nymann. Steinman is accompanied by three high-ranking butchers' union officers and two union lawyers.

One of the lawyers, Harold I. Cammer, is an outside counsel hired to defend the union against lawsuits brought against it by Iowa Beef. Cammer is confounded by the assemblage in the hotel room. He says later that Steinman "was just a furtive-looking character out of *Guys and Dolls*. I thought he was a messenger or a coffee-getter. Some greasy, sleazy-looking fellow who never looked you in the eye, who had a hang-dog look about him. I thought he was there to get coffee for the Iowa Beef people. I had no notion until later that I was in the presence of a famous character. . . . This fellow, he looks like a worm." But in contrast, Cammer says, the Iowa Beef executives "looked like a bunch of Texas rangers."

Neither Holman nor Steinman knows that a crack squad of detectives from the New York district attorney's office is planning to throw wiretaps around Steinman's operations in hope that the taps will obtain evidence to imprison the corruptors in the meat industry. For what they do in this room today, Currier Holman and Moe Steinman will be indicted by a New York grand jury for conspiring to bribe union officials and supermarket chain executives. They will be accused of plotting to pay these bribes with money from unnecessary meat brokerage commissions of more than $1 million a year. Steinman will plead guilty to this and other crimes in exchange for stunningly lenient treatment. Holman will plead innocent and face a six-week trial.

What follows is the story of how a well-scrubbed, all-American boy from the Midwest wound up in a bed of New York hoodlums. The story is told from thousands of pages of trial testimony and other court documents, and from numerous interviews. Although Holman refused to be interviewed on any subject for this report, and did not testify at his trial, his secretly tape-recorded version of the whole story, given in the district attorney's office, was submitted into evidence at the trial.

Currier Holman—Currier is his mother's family name—was born in 1911 in Sioux City, Iowa, an area his grandfather had helped pioneer. Holman's father had accumulated enough holdings in real estate and banks so that neighbors considered the Holmans well-to-do, although family members reject that description. The elder Holman died in a flu epidemic in 1918. Currier moved with the rest of the family to California. His elementary school was Hitchcock Military Academy in San Rafael. After that he was packed off to prep school at Shattuck Military Academy in Faribault, Minnesota, where his mother had attended a sister school. About his private schooling, Dr. Clifford Bowers, a lifelong friend, says, "His mother was kind of a socialite and those things were kind of important to her."

Holman's entry in *Who's Who in America* lists his education as Notre Dame, Class of 1933. Notre Dame says it parted company with Holman for undisclosed reasons during his junior year in 1932. Grant Holman says his brother Currier quit college in disappointment after a broken appendix forced an end to his football career in 1932. George Henry Rohrs, who really was graduated from Notre Dame in 1933, says Holman's football career was ended in 1930 by none other than George Henry Rohrs. According to Rohrs, "I beat him out, I'd say," for the final remaining spot on the varsity, the last team ever coached by Knute Rockne, who died the next year.

"I remember him because we played the same position (end)," Rohrs says, but adds, "I wouldn't say that many people would remember him. He didn't make a big impression then. That's why I was surprised to see (in a recent newspaper article) how prominent a position he held. He was a big, strong farm boy, and those people keep to themselves pretty well." Talks with other classmates bear out the picture of Holman's inconspicuousness as a collegian.

After leaving Notre Dame, Holman briefly attended the University of Oklahoma. He left to get married. The marriage was annulled after eight months. A few years later he met and married a Sioux City woman who remains Mrs. Holman to this day.

Meanwhile, even in the depths of the Depression, the Holman name carried enough influence in Sioux City to land Holman a job, albeit a dirty one, friends say. He was hired by Swift and Company and sent to what was known as the "gut shanty" at the Swift plant, where his job was stripping the offal from freshly slaughtered carcasses.

Even back in those days, friends remember Holman talking incessantly about the inefficiencies he saw. The cattle he was helping slaughter had spent several days en route from the feed lots where they were fattened, and perhaps another day in the pens where they were bought and sold. The wasted time and extra handling resulted in considerable weight loss. The slaughtering operation itself seemed inefficiently organized. And many live cattle were being shipped in railroad boxcars to distant slaughterhouses on the east and west coasts, resulting not only in weight loss but in much greater shipping, slaughtering and butchering costs than if the kill had been made at a central location. Grant Holman remembers his brother, while still in the gut shanty at Swift, talking about the packing house he would start one day. "I want to be the biggest packer in the world," Currier Holman told his family then.

After several years, Swift put Holman into office work, but four months later he left. Armour had offered him the job he really wanted—buying cattle.

Holman saved his money, and early in the war years he found an opportunity to buy into an established private cattle trading concern at the Sioux City stockyards. A few

131

years later, his partner retired and Holman was on his own. Soon he became the biggest cattle trader in one of the biggest stockyards in the country.

Recalls his friend Dr. Bowers, "As an order buyer you can work as many hours as you want and make as much money as you want. He was there fifteen or eighteen hours a day, seven days a week. If anybody wanted to buy cattle, Currier was there to sell them." Another lifelong acquaintance, Neil Tennis, an Iowa banker, adds, "Nobody would work as hard as Currier. A thirty-six-hour day wouldn't be long enough for him. He eats and breathes this stuff. We run into him socially late at night, and that's all he can talk about. We can start talking baseball, but it always gets back to the cattle business."

Holman's intense concentration on work made life difficult for some of those around him. "The family isn't happy," says one close relative. "They don't have a father, they've got a business. He has very few friends because he talks nothing but business, constantly."

For fifteen years Holman took phone calls from small slaughterhouses around the U.S. and bought cattle in the Sioux City yards to fill their orders. But through all that time he never lost the dream of one day starting his own packing company. Finally, in 1953, he began knocking on doors, looking for financing.

His idea of challenging old-line packing companies with up-to-date methods was not entirely novel in Sioux City. Says Dr. Bowers, who became one of Holman's investors, "Quite a few people had thought of it but nobody had been willing to gamble on it. The general idea was that it would fail because Armour, Cudahy and Swift were so big." Over the next two years, Holman managed to convince some twenty-five to thirty Sioux City burghers to lay out about $1 million, of which Mr. Holman himself put up about $50,000, friends say.

His new firm, Sioux City Dressed Beef, started operations in 1955. Its style was adventuresome for its day, but

far from the revolutionary style that Iowa Beef would cut a
decade later. At Sioux City Dressed Beef there were the
beginnings of an assembly line. A conveyor chain brought
the cattle after slaughter past rows of workmen who
methodically hacked the carcass into quarters. Thus Holman pioneered two of his ideas: the use of what he calls
"General Motors technology," where each butcher in line
performs a specific function as the carcass moves past instead of the old way of having one man prepare each carcass; and the shipping of beef in quarters instead of in
trimmed carcasses, eliminating much waste material from
shipping. Neither idea, however, was carried anywhere
close to its ultimate conclusion.

One reason for Sioux City Dressed Beef's limited success, both financial and technological, was Holman's unwillingness to bet all his chips on it at the start. Instead of
running the plant himself, Holman had his investors hire a
professional manager. He continued full-time in his
cattle-selling business, which seemed a neat, if in some
minds questionable, idea. According to sources who would
know, he had a hammerlock on the business of a major new
cattle-buyer—Sioux City Dressed Beef. Thus, apparently
he stood to profit from the new packinghouse's cash flow as
a supplier even if he didn't as an investor. (Holman didn't
respond when this was given to his office for comment.)

Within a few years Holman and his professional manager
were feuding, and many of the investors sided with the
manager. Ostensibly, the issues were such matters as
whether to branch out into pork (Holman argued that his
innovations were geared specifically to beef). But basically, in the words of one person who was close to the
company, the issue was that "Currier Holman isn't going to
be involved in something without wanting to run the
whole show himself."

Holman and the investors who sided with him were
bought out by their partners and eventually the manager
acquired control. The plant they founded is still operating

in Sioux City, though it has been through several changes of name and ownership.

After giving up on Sioux City Dressed Beef, Holman went back to ringing doorbells of potential investors in hopes of founding a new packing house. Meanwhile, he had made friends with his future partner, A. D. (Andy) Anderson. Anderson had built a pork plant in nearby Dennison, Iowa, in the mid-1950s and already shared Holman's opinions about the need to redesign the packing process to take advantage of modern technology.

According to a story Holman told in 1974 to Ellen Fleysher, a reporter with WCBS-TV in New York, Anderson used to run a small store and "on Thursday nights Andy would be down in the dumps" because that night he'd have "to scale all those fish" for the Friday trade. Then came frozen, prescaled fish. Although they yielded a lower profit margin on each sale, frozen fish eliminated the mess and brought an increase in volume. They represented the inevitable march of progress. Why shouldn't the same system work with beef? "You know," Anderson would tell Holman, who latched onto the phrase himself, "you can't go back to scalin' fish on Thursday night."

They decided to found a new packing company, and by 1960 they got the money, mostly with the help of investors who had sided with Holman in selling interests in Sioux City Dressed Beef. Iowa Beef Processors Inc. opened its first plant in May 1961, in Dennison, with Holman and Anderson as co-chairmen.

Although the great technological leap forward was still in the future, the Dennison plant did represent an important advance. Holman purchased cattle directly from feedlot owners near Dennison, thus thumbing his nose at industry practice. The rules of the Sioux City Stockyards said that all cattle had to be brought to the stockyards and sold there. But Holman saw that this ritual held up the slaughter for several days and caused a weight loss of up to 7 percent. Since Holman no longer was a member of the stockyards and was buying only for his own company, he made his own arrangements with feed-lot owners. Cattle were brought in just when the assembly-line process was ready to gobble them up. As soon as two or three hours after the animal left the grain trough, the knife descended. (Some packing houses had begun buying cattle direct from the feed lot before Holman got started, but Iowa Beef greatly quickened the trend.)

To make this system succeed, Iowa Beef needed a series of processing plants, each near a feed lot. Holman and Anderson purchased a second plant in Fort Dodge, Iowa, remodeled it to their assembly line system, and opened it in June 1962. By 1975, there were nine Iowa Beef plants. (Iowa Beef still buys some cattle through the Sioux City stockyards, and when it does, it often buys them through Holman's old firm, which now is known as United Order Buyers. Raymond Lynch, who used to be Holman's partner and now says he is sole owner, insists that Holman has no financial interest remaining in the firm.)

In the early 1960s, Holman and Anderson knew very well where they were headed. If it made sense to reduce the carcass to quarters before shipping it out of the Midwest, then it made more sense to reduce it to primal cuts (loins, ribs, shoulders, etc.) and eventually to individual cooking portions, wrapped in the same plastic trays that the east coast housewife ultimately would take off her supermarket meat counter.

The first obstacle—the only one Holman and Anderson seemed aware of at first—was technology. To ship such small cuts they would need new processes for butchering, sealing and freezing the meat. The processes called for materials and equipment that didn't exist yet.

From about 1962, they began working with manufacturers to design the stuff they'd need. For example, Iowa Beef guided Dow Chemical toward development of a new kind of plastic wrapper that would handle easily, seal in the meat from contamination and yet allow it to continue aging in transit. With machine tool manufacturers, Iowa Beef designed a variety of special saws that would allow assembly line butchers to conduct their individual operations quickly and neatly as the conveyor belt moved on. Holman and Anderson laid out a plant in which steers would be reduced to primal cuts, which would be frozen in plastic and boxed.

Instead of receiving a swinging carcass, the purchaser would receive a box of what he wanted. A & P could hold a sale on chuck in New York while Safeway held a sale on rump roast—from the same cow— in San Francisco. The butchering process would be much more efficient at a central location. Byproducts that the supermarkets couldn't use, such as bone (which is ground up for animal food) and hide, could be disposed of centrally, which benefitted cost control and ecology.

The first of these revolutionary meat plants opened in Dakota City, Nebraska, early in 1967, for boxing ribs and loins. It took two more years to bring it to where it could process an entire steer as Holman had dreamed, and by then a second such plant was under construction at Emporia, Kansas. Says one Iowa Beef executive who worked directly under Holman and Anderson, "Instead of having to teach every operator how to do a whole lot of things, they now have to teach an operator only how to do one thing, such as bone out a plate. The next operator does something else. One man with a certain kind of saw separates the head loin from the short loin. Then it goes to another operation where a guy with a hand knife separates out the tenderloin. Then another operator on a saw saws the bone off the strip loin to make it a boneless strip." And so on.

By 1969, Holman and his associates seemed to have the technology well in hand. It would be only a few more years before they carried their process to its logical conclusion and packaged each individual cooking portion of meat at a central location, so that all a supermarket needed to do was unpack a box. But there was one element they hadn't reckoned with: the Amalgamated Meat Cutters and Retail Clerks union.

Although Holman argues that his process saves money on shipping costs, the expense of cutting up, freezing and sealing the meat largely offsets this saving (and some supermarket executives say it more than offsets savings). There is, however, one way that Holman's process indisputably can shrink the retail price of meat: the process eliminates butchers' jobs at warehouses and retail stores.

On August 24 1969, just before the costly new Emporia plant was to open, the butchers' union struck, ostensibly over local issues. But Holman was quick to see, or think he saw, the union's real motive. By the fall of 1969, the union, calling Iowa Beef "the monster of the industry," had spread its strike activity from the home plant in Dakota City across the country.

According to what Holman later told the district attorney's men and their hidden tape recorder, the strike occasioned seventy felonies, hundreds of misdemeanors and one murder; "and finally they burnt our general counsel's house to the ground. It was intended to be my house, which is immediately contiguous to his, but they just missed."

Holman commiserated with Anderson. "It became obvious," he told the D.A., "that we, a couple of naive Midwesterners . . . didn't really understand. Every Amalgamated contract in the country has a clause which says that they'll only take carcass beef. Now several years ago we decided we might someday take that to the Supreme Court, because it might be an illegal part of any contract. Bu we didn't choose to do that before we built millions of dollars worth of facilities."

To move his boxed beef into New York markets, Holman made deals with Supermarkets General (the Pathmark chain) and the Wakefern cooperative (which services the

Shoprite chain). But after the first half-dozen carloads, Iowa Beef's shipments were turned back. Supermarket executives remarked about poor quality, but Iowa Beef officials, convinced their quality was excellent, blamed the butchers' union for refusing to handle boxed meat. Holman's company filed suit against the union, alleging illegal secondary boycotts. But the court process is slow, and the lack of income to pay debts threatened to turn Holman's empire belly up.

Then, in October 1969, at the height of the strike/boycott crisis, Holman received a phone call from Benny Moscowitz, a New York meat wholesaler he had dealt with back in the 1940s. Moscowitz told Holman that there were some "people . . . you've got to meet. I'll bring them out." Not having seen Moscowitz in years, Holman didn't know that his old acquaintance was now working with Moe Steinman. (Although Moscowitz wasn't charged in a criminal case, one indictment that grew out of the scandal lists him as a payer of bribes with Steinman to supermarket executives).

So out to Sioux City came Moe Steinman. Even at their first meeting there, Holman learned of Steinman's distaste for doing business in offices, and his preference for restaurants, hostelries and coin telephone booths.

"And so we're sitting in the middle of the lobby of a motel," Holman recalls, "and I said, 'What are you? What's your business? What do you want to talk about?' He says, 'Er, I do a couple of things.'"

Actually, Steinman did more than a couple of things. Ostensibly employed for many years as vice president, labor relations, for the Daitch-Shopwell supermarket chain (Shopwell Inc.), that title hardly explained his influence. He also invested in business deals with the heads of the labor unions he negotiated with; he operated numerous meat brokerages that sold to various supermarket chains, including his own; he paid back part of the brokerage fees to supermarket executives or their relatives; he negotiated labor disputes for other supermarket chains and meat companies, and he was a companion of Mafia captain and sometimes kosher meat purveyor John (Johnny Dio) Dioguardi.

Prominent persons in the New York meat industry say that Steinman's power hasn't been absolute. Many wholesalers have stayed successfully in business for years, although they deny paying commissions to one of his brokerages. But his influence has been astounding. Almost everyone in the industry seems to know him, and many a business deal has been altered out of respect for him.

Fear has been one incentive. In 1972, Sheldon Epstein, a New York meat wholesaler, was shot dead by an unidentified gunman at a Manhattan bar shortly after making plans with two other men to start a farm-to-counter veal business. Their business would have competed with leading firms that paid commissions to a brokerage run by Moe Steinman and his brother Sol. The police, who never mentioned the prospective veal business in public if they even knew about it, speculated openly that a Mafia hit man had mistaken Epstein for a mobster who had been at the bar earlier.

But some persons in the meat industry were impressed otherwise. The head of one large meat firm, after mentioning the shooting, says he knows of other industry figures who "wound up in cement shoes" for getting out of line. He won't go into detail because, he says, "I don't want to wind up in a box." Many other dealers also are close-mouthed. "It's not themselves they're afraid for so much," one says, "it's their families."

Fear aside, there has been plenty of profit for men in the meat industry who do business the Steinman way. Some twelve supermarket executives were indicted after the recent meat investigation on charges that they evaded federal income tax, or filed falsely, in connection with bribes from Steinman and his associates. In many cases, according to the indictments, the bribes ranged around $100,000 a year to each executive, although some recipients may have split their lucre with a colleague or two. At this writing, nine of the executives have pleaded guilty and three are awaiting trial.

Chains named in the indictments as being under Steinman's influence, though the chains themselves weren't indicted, included Food City, Bohack, Hill's, Waldbaum's, First National, Big Apple, Wakefern, Food-o-Rama, Sloan's and King Kullen. Some relatives of supermarket executives were on the allegedly padded payrolls of Steinman's brokerages, and sources say they received as much as $250 a week.

The son of Herbert Newman, one Steinman brokerage partner, also was on the list of allegedly phony employes. New York City detectives reportedly saw the son relieving a safety deposit box of more than $200,000 in bonds one day.

In 1972 grand jury testimony, later made public, Herbert Newman was questioned about $78,000 in supermarket brokerage fees missing from the Steinman-Newman meat firm in one two-month period. A prosecutor said it seemed "clear" from the conversation that the $78,000 had gone as "payoffs to the mob elements," specifically Tommy Dio, brother of Johnny Dio. Replied Newman, "I can't say that he (Steinman) went and gave this to the Mob . . . I know that he knows them all. I know he associates with them. . . . I never was there." Newman was indicted on eight counts of giving "conspicuously unbelievable, evasive, equivocal and patently false" answers in his testimony, but he has been reported too ill from cancer to stand trial.

Other money from Steinman's commissions allegedly has gone to officials of the butchers' union to promote "labor peace." At this writing, three officials of the union in the New York area are awaiting trial on charges that they took, and didn't report on their income-tax returns, about $5,000 a month, plus occasional thousands in bonuses, from Steinman and several supermarket officials under his influence.

A series of telephone conversations in 1971, wiretapped by New York police and later made public, tell how Steinman would get involved in labor and management affairs. Food-o-Rama, a chain whose shares were traded on the American Stock Exchange, had suddenly stopped buying meat from the Steinman-Newman brokerage. Soon, George George, senior vice-president at Food-o-Rama, received a telephone call from Jules Tantleff, a former Bohack supermarket executive who had taken over a classy Manhattan restaurant business from two butchers' union officials and who was a longtime friend of Steinman's. Tantleff explained to George that Moe Steinman, the meat broker and Daitch-Shopwell executive, "could be helpful in an advisory capacity" in Food-o-Rama's upcoming union negotiations. In exchange, George was told, it would certainly be nice if Food-o-Rama resumed purchases from Mr. Steinman's brokerage. Tantleff would receive a share of Steinman's commissions and would kick back a portion to George for his trouble. According to grand jury testimony, George got about $700 a month and shared it with another Food-o-Rama executive. At Steinman's request, Tantleff also persuaded George to switch Food-o-Rama's purchases of frozen meat patties to a brand sold by a Steinman associate—the same Ben Moscowitz who later would introduce Steinman to Holman.

Meanwhile, Food-o-Rama's labor negotiations started. George would relay his company's wishes through Tantleff (the restaurant owner and former Bohack officer) to Steinman. Steinman would talk the proposals over with two butchers' union officers, Nicholas Abondolo and Irving Stern, both of whom at this writing are awaiting trial on charges that they failed to pay income tax on large payoffs they allegedly received regularly from Steinman. After his talks with the union leaders, Steinman would send back instructions via Tantleff on exactly what George was to say

141

and do during the negotiations—even as to when he should go to the door. Repeated throughout the wiretapped discussions is the phrase, "tell the truth"—apparently a euphemism in the Steinman fraternity for paying people off.

The tradeoffs at Food-o-Rama are just one example of many similar goings-on described in the thousands of pages of grand jury testimony, wiretap transcripts and indictments that were produced in the New York district attorney's investigation into meat industry corruption. Steinman involved himself in the labor affairs of still other supermarket chains.

In one wiretapped conversation, Tantleff told Sol Steinman, Moe's brother and partner, how he used to handle bribery back when he was an officer at Bohack. "I used to handle it personally," Tantleff explained. "Then I'd put in expense vouchers over a period of two or three months to get it back."

(In 1974, Tantleff and George were brought to trial for their activities. When all charges against them had been adjudicated, Tantleff was convicted of criminal contempt and sentenced to a maximum jail term of four months; George pleaded guilty to false swearing before the grand jury and was fined $500.)

This was the world that Steinman brought to Holman in the motel lobby in Sioux City late in 1969. Of course, Steinman didn't explain all the intricacies of the system right away. When Holman asked his occupation, Steinman mentioned merely that he was vice-president, labor relations, for Daitch-Shopwell, and that he was a partner in Trans-World Fabricators, a meat brokerage.

Holman: "I said, 'Well, that's interesting. . . . What the hell—er—how can you be a vice president for Daitch-Shopwell?. . . You know, you couldn't work for me.' I said, 'We don't countenance people doing two or three things on the side. . . .' Well, he laughed it off. . . . I said, 'We're trying to sell a lot of meat to the chain stores. We tried to sell your goddamned chain. Maybe you can help us out.'

"He said, 'Maybe I can.'"

Soon Holman was talking to Herbie Newman, managing partner in Trans-World Fabricators. "We're getting killed with boycotts in New York," Holman complained. "If you can move any goddamned meat, why we'll sure appreciate it." Then came several calls from Moscowitz, during which he would put on the phone men he identified as former vice presidents of butchers' union locals. Holman was impressed. But the strike and the butchers' blockade against boxed beef continued.

Early in April 1970, Iowa Beef's New York bankers threatened to call the strike-bound company's credit line. If they did, Holman says, Iowa Beef would have "gone broke." Faced with a dire need to break into the world's largest meat market, Holman says, "Andy (Anderson) and I decided to come. . . to New York City and talk to Mr. Steinman."

About this time, P. L. Nymann, Iowa Beef's general counsel, remembers Holman commenting about how "Mr. Steinman had influence with or could handle union officers. . . . I wasn't sure whether it meant that he'd wine them and dine them or do other favors for them or possibly the ultimate of paying them money," Nymann says.

Hardly had the decision been made to go to New York than the strike at the Dakota City plant ended, on April 13. On April 21, Holman, Anderson and Nymann checked into the Stanhope Hotel in Manhattan and called Moe Steinman. He came over with his brother Sol and partner Newman. Holman said Iowa Beef needed to sell sixteen thousand carcasses of boxed beef a week in the New York area, more than anybody ever had sold before. Steinman whipped out the Yellow Pages and pointed out fourteen supermarket chains that, according to Holman, "he thought he could help us with."

Then Holman brought up the union opposition. "I know," Steinman replied, "but I think I can handle it."

Holman: "He went to the corner phone, made three or four calls . . . and then two people called him back. . . . He said, okay, he said, tomorrow noon we'll have the . . . presidents of the unions that are involved in this . . . here and we'll talk."

Sure enough, at noon the next day, Steinman knocked at the Iowa Beef suite at the Stanhope and led the executives down the hall to another suite. There they found waiting three high-ranking butchers' officers, Irving Kaplan, Irving Stern and Albert DeProspoe, and two union lawyers. (Stern is one of three butchers' union officials who have pleaded guilty to evading taxes on large bribes from Steinman and other supermarket officials. At this writing they are awaiting sentencing.)

In the darkened room, the opposing lawyers began to debate the boycott suits, when suddenly Stern, the union's director of organization, bellowed, "You goddamned lawyers get the hell out of here! You get your ass out and don't come back till I call you." The lawyers left.

"What's the deal?" Stern then demanded. Holman said he wanted to get his boxed beef into New York and would be willing to drop Iowa Beef's multimillion-dollar suits against the union if it would agree not to fight boxed beef. Steinman told the Iowa Beef men to go back to their own suite for awhile. About ninety minutes later he called them back in. "If you do what you say you're going to do, you got it," he proclaimed.

According to Holman, the lawyers, on hearing that their big litigation was finished, seemed about "to cry—or jump out the window." But Holman argued that he wanted to sell beef, not bust the union treasuries in court.

Then, according to Howard Weiner, Iowa Beef's financial vice president and treasurer at the time, a union officer "recommended or suggested or identified" Steinman as "a person who could help Iowa Beef with its boxed beef program in New York. . . . His influence was with meat people and with union people."

144

The upshot: Over drinks at the Stanhope bar, the Iowa Beef men agreed to pay Steinman's Trans-World brokerage twenty-five cents for every hundred pounds of Iowa Beef's boxed meat sold within a 125-mile radius of Columbus Circle, near the center of Manhattan. Then Steinman and his brother Sol took the Iowa Beef men to dinner at the Black Angus Restaurant, where, according to testimony, Steinman had boasted that he paid off butchers' union officers the first Tuesday of every month, and where he sometimes met with his Mafia friend John (Johnny Dio) Dioguardi.

(For several decades the Black Angus has been the center of an elaborate web of interconnections. In recent years it has been owned by Jules Tantleff, the former Bohack executive. He bought it from Louis and Max Block, former officials of the butchers' union. The Block brothers also owned a country club in Connecticut, which they bought with money from the sale of bonds to investors like Moe Steinman and several other supermarket executives. Max Block also was connected with a kosher provision company that sold to supermarket chains, including Daitch-Shopwell, through meat brokers, including Moe Steinman. Johnny Dio was another employee of the same kosher provision company after his release from prison, where he served time for extortion, fraud and state and federal tax violations.)

After the Iowa Beef officials returned to Dakota City, they had misgivings. Weiner, the financial vice-president, remembers "many, many meetings" discussing the "curious . . . nature of (Steinman's) relationship with the union . . . This seemed in conflict of what we were used to (in) management people." The talk was, he says, "that Moe Steinman's influence and his ability to open doors meant that he was going to pay off union people and meat buyers. This possibility was distasteful to everyone in these meetings, including Mr. Holman. . . .

"I heard said at various times, 'It's a sad state of affairs that Iowa Beef, (then) the 127th largest manufacturing company in the country, the largest beef producer in the world, has to do business with people like this.' Mr. Holman agreed. (But) the conversations always came to a conclusion by Mr. Holman's question: 'Do you want to get your meat into New York? New York is the largest meat market in the world. You want to sell there or don't you?' "

The executives telephoned the chairman of Holly Farms, the nation's largest chicken purveyor. He reportedly told them that he, too, had been unable to sell in New York before he signed a brokerage agreement with Moe Steinman.

Within a month, Moe and Sol Steinman flew to Dakota City, where Holman was disappointed that they showed no interest in receiving a grand tour of the most wonderful meat plant in the whole world. Instead, they brought Holman some bad news.

First, they said, they would need a commission of fifty cents a hundred pounds instead of twenty-five cents to move the boxed beef.

Holman: "I said, 'For Christ's sake, I'm not going to pay fifty cents a hundred . . . ' " Mr. Steinman replied: "Well, look, I need the fifty cents. I got to buy a union steward. You had trouble in Supermarkets General? I've got to buy a guy a broad. I may have to buy a chain-store buyer. I've got to pay cash."

The fee was left hanging. But there was more bad news. Contrary to Iowa Beef's expectation, Steinman didn't plan to invest in cooling and warehousing facilities to handle the beef. He would open doors, but moving and storing the meat was Iowa's Beef's problem. Iowa Beef president Roy Lee Jr. recalls that the executives recognized Steinman was going to do very little for his money under the brokerage agreement, but they figured his payoffs would make the deal work anyway.

"Jesus Christ," Holman says Anderson told him. 'You know what we did in Las Vegas? We can't sell a goddamned pound of meat out there. You know what (another man) said about (a large hotel in Los Angeles)—we got to buy the goddamned chef in order to get meat in there.'

"And I concurred," Holman says. "We're going to pay (Steinman) just as cheap as we can," he told the other executives, "but look, we got to get New York." Iowa Beef, he said, was "dealing with a bunch of crooks in New York, (the) same crooks we deal with in Los Angeles, or you have them out in Las Vegas or . . . well, specifically Moe Steinman and all the rest of the people. Anybody that's in the meat business in New York is a crook."

Nymann, the general counsel, says he tried to protest that the plan was dangerous, even illegal, but Holman interrupted him. "I know that you lawyers would tell us not to do this," Nymann quoted Holman as saying, "but I'm going to do it anyway."

When Steinman returned to New York, he instructed Louis Jacobs, the Iowa Beef sales executive, to rent an office for a new brokerage firm to handle the Iowa Beef account. The firm was called Cattle Pakt Sales Inc., later shortened to C. P. Sales Inc., and the office was at Fifty-sixth Street and Madison Avenue, rather far from the grubby area south of Fourteenth Street, where most meat brokerages operate.

Jacobs says he would call Steinman early in the morning at his home and ask for appointments with supermarket buyers. Steinman would call back with an appointment schedule. But Steinman didn't go to the meetings, and normally his name wouldn't come up. He said it "wasn't necessary" to mention his name to the buyers, Jacobs recalls.

On June 3, Jacobs visited Aaron Freedman, meat executive for Waldbaum's, a regional chain. Freedman expressed interest in boxed beef, but said, "I'm going to have to speak to Moe Steinman about it." (Freedman's death prevented his indictment after the scandal broke; authorities considered him one of the biggest bribe-takers in the area.) Eventually, Freedman and Steinman flew together to Dakota City to meet Holman, and Waldbaum's became Iowa Beef's long-sought "showcase" customer in New York and suburbs. Apparently, there was no union opposition.

Also on June 3, Jacobs visited the Big Apple chain, where Alvin Bernstein, the meat executive, gave him the same reply: Big Apple wouldn't buy meat until Moe Steinman, the vice-president of the rival Daitch-Shopwell chain, approved. On June 15, Jacobs met Steinman, and the next day, apparently as a result, he met Bernstein, who placed an order.

On Wednesday, July 8, Jacobs went to Food Fair. "They told me that as in the past they had no clearance from their local union for permission to handle boxed beef. I called Moe Steinman and told him about it, and he said that he would . . . take care of it." Steinman didn't take care of it alone; he went to Food Fair with Iving Kaplan, the union official, to make his pitch. Kaplan was used to making pitches. Back in the 1960s, still a butchers' union officer, he made sales pitches to supermarkets for a detergent backed by a Mafia figure.

After refusing to buy the detergent, several A & P properties were firebombed, and a store manager was shot dead.

Jacobs later wrote back to Holman, "Until the time that Moe and Mr. Kaplan cleared the way, Food Fair had never taken the boxed product . . . " It did then. C. P. Sales also sold to Hill's, where the order was placed by buying agents Blase Iovino, Sal Coletta and George Gamaldi.

Barnett Freedman, Aaron Freedman's brother and also an executive at Waldbaum's, has since pleaded guilty to tax evasion in connection with an indictment accusing him of taking $43,000 in bribes on meat purchases. (Aaron Freedman reportedly received much more.) Alvin Bernstein of Big Apple, and another Big Apple executive, have pleaded guilty to tax evasion in connection with an indictment accusing them of taking bribes that in Bernstein's case reached more than $170,000 in 1970 alone. Iovino and Coletta at this writing are awaiting trial on charges that they concealed bribes of $297,800 and $306,174 respectively on their tax returns. Charges against Gamaldi were dismissed.

When the New York district attorney's office and the federal Strike Force against organized crime investigated, they found careful records indicating that none of the money Iowa Beef paid to C. P. Sales was relayed as bribes. The alleged bribes all came from other Steinman-linked brokerages that had no direct dealings with Iowa Beef. So Holman and Iowa Beef were charged only with conspiracy to bribe, not with actual bribery, even though other indictments say that the same supermarket officials who were buying Iowa Beef's meat were well taken care of by Steinman and his associates.

In December 1970, Steinman renewed his demand for a fifty-cent commission rate, and insisted on a contract in perpetuity on all Iowa Beef products sold in the New York area. He was rejecting any requirement that he sell a certain quota of beef. So the Iowa Beef executives piled into their private jet and rendezvoused with their man Moe in another New York hotel, this time the Hawthorne House. The meeting lasted until about 4:30 A.M. on December 5.

When Weiner, the vice-president, complained that fifty cents was too high, Steinman "stated to me that he had certain expenses that others didn't have. . . . I asked him what those expenses were. And he said, 'Well, I have income tax'—and I interrupted him and said, 'Everyone has that. That's not unusual.' He said, 'Well, kid, I have other expenses, too. There are three kinds. I pay meat buyers off at 15 percent. I pay union people off at 7 percent. And it costs me 10 percent to convert the corporate money to cash, and I have to deal in cash.' I said I understood."

Holman remembers the expense accounting a little differently. He says Steinman contended he had to pay a full one-third of his commission to union officials, another third to chain-store executives, and that taxes ate up most of the rest. (Steinman, however, was indicted for tax fraud.)

Weiner remembers lots of shouting at the meeting. Steinman finally settled for a fee of fifty cents a hundred pounds for the first five million pounds of boxed beef moved each month, and thirty-five cents thereafter. But only on one condition. Steinman turned to Walter Bodenstein, his son-in-law, a New York lawyer who had been sitting quietly through the meeting. Then, in Weiner's words, Steinman "suggested to Mr. Holman that Walter Bodenstein . . . could be invaluable to Iowa Beef in the New York area for some of their legal problems if and when they had them. He knew lots of union people, did a lot of legal work for union people and others, and suggested that Iowa Beef put him on a retainer."

Holman had heard of Bodenstein before. The previous summer, when he had called the chairman of Holly Farms to inquire about Steinman, he had been told, "You probably may have to hire his son-in-law in the bargain, but the kid's a good kid." Steinman was asking a retainer of $50,000 a year for Bodenstein. Holman agreed to pay $25,000. According to Lee, it was the first time Iowa Beef had retained legal counsel outside Dakota City.

As the time came for the agreement to be reduced to a formal contract, Steinman announced that he was bowing out of C. P. Sales and Iowa Beef meat brokering and that Bodenstein was taking over.

The contract was signed in January 1971. Soon Steinman had hired a professional manager to work under Bodenstein, who also had a large staff to train supermarkets in how to use boxed beef, although the staff mostly was paid by Iowa Beef rather than out of C. P. Sales's brokerage commissions. Another Steinman son-in-law, Nat Myerson, was treasurer. At one point, Bodenstein wanted to take C. P. Sales public with a stock offering. Its registration would have ballyhooed its five-year exclusive contract with Iowa

Beef. Iowa Beef persuaded Bodenstein to shelve these plans.

Whether Steinman's influence continued to guide his son-in-law became a legal issue. The indictment against Iowa Beef and Holman came down in March 1973, more than two years after Steinman announced he was quitting. The statute of limitations on conspiracy is only two years. That was one of the two main defenses that Iowa Beef and Holman put up at their trial in the summer of 1974. The other defense was that there wasn't any conspiracy even before January 1971, because Holman never actually believed that Steinman was bribing anybody, but only that he was dickering for a higher commission.

The prosecution said that Steinman did remain as part of the conspiracy, and will remain part of it at least until January 1976, because, at Iowa Beef's insistence, he signed the five-year contract in January 1971. Iowa Beef and Holman said that they asked for Steinman's signature only to guarantee that he wouldn't start another brokerage business to help a competing beef firm.

In conversation later in 1971 with an Iowa Beef executive, and after that in a letter to Iowa Beef, Bodenstein denied that he had ever agreed to or intended to bribe anyone. As to Steinman's statements in the hotel room, which Mr. Bodenstein had listened to, Bodenstein said simply that his father-in-law "talked too much." Iowa Beef executives reacted with great surprise to this line from Bodenstein. Whether he adopted it before or after he learned that C. P. Sales was under investigation isn't clear.

By the time the indictments came down early in 1973, Holman had fired Howard Weiner and Roy Lee. P. L. Nymann had resigned and Andy Anderson also had departed. Nymann and Weiner say their departures were caused specifically by strong disagreements with Holman about what they would tell the grand jury. Says Nymann, the former general counsel, "I didn't feel that I could participate in the investigation where it seemed that people were going to say that they didn't remember the events of a significant meeting." Weiner says that Holman exploded in obscenities upon learning that Weiner had told "everything" when interviewed by attorneys in New York.

In July and August 1974, New York State Supreme Court Judge Burton B. Roberts, at Holman's choice without a jury, tried the case of Currier Holman and Iowa Beef Processors Inc. At the time of trial, Judge Roberts had turned down a plea of guilty by Moe Steinman to corresponding conspiracy charges; Judge Roberts said he was dissatisfied with Steinman's unwillingness to make a broad confession of the facts of the crime.

After more than a month of deliberating, Judge Roberts found Holman and Iowa Beef guilty, but cloaked his decision with reluctance. Of Holman, Judge Roberts said in his decision, "He knew that payoffs had to be made on behalf of (Iowa Beef) to sell its meat in other areas. He was also very much aware that payoffs were considered a necessary cost of doing business in the New York City retail meat trade. He had been in the meat business too long and had come too far not to have seen the handwriting on the wall. It is naive to think that he would allow the fate of the company he built, but which was now so perilously close to ruin, to hinge on the possible success of an honest-to-goodness salesman who had to pound the pavement and knock on doors in hopes of finding a meat buyer who was not already 'on the take' and convincing him of the merits of boxed beef. (Iowa Beef's) survival depended on someone to sell their meat who was capable of satisfying the 'crooks,' as he called them, in the New York market. The tribute the unions and buyers were apparently receiving from everyone else would have to be paid by (Iowa Beef) as well. . . . Somewhat to his credit, it was not until the company was on the brink of fiscal disaster that he agreed to pay the price. . . . Sadly, like a modern day Dr. Faustus, Currier J. Holman sold his soul to Moe Steinman."

The wrath that Judge Roberts refused to visit on Holman, he delivered instead to the state and federal prosecutors who he said were offering lenient treatment to Steinman, whom he called a "barracuda," in order to convict Holman, whom he referred to as a "minnow." In light of this, he meted out to Holman an unconditional discharge, no punishment whatsoever, and to Iowa Beef a $7,000 fine.

Iowa Beef's net profit in its fiscal year ending November 2 1974 was $16.4 million on sales of $1.54 billion. According to an attorney for Walter Bodenstein, C. P. Sales was continuing to receive commissions from Iowa Beef at the rate of more than $1 million a year even while the bribery/conspiracy trial was going on. Both Holman and Iowa Beef are appealing their convictions.

Steinman's guilty plea, under the deal arranged for him by the prosecutors, was finally accepted by another judge. Judge Roberts bowed out of the case, saying he could not have tried Steinman fairly after hearing the Holman case.

In the summer of 1975, Steinman began serving a federal prison term that cannot exceed one year and that probably will be over in much less. Meat industry sources say that his former associates are continuing his operations.

As so often happens, after law enforcement officials had finished dickering with each other over which criminals would get off easy to help insure stiff punishment for other criminals, all the criminals wound up getting off easy. As of this writing, the stiffest prison term imposed on any of the supermarket executives convicted in the scandal was four months, with most of the executives getting suspended sentences or probation, despite the purported aid of Steinman in their prosecution.

Currier Holman seems unchanged by his experience. In November, 1975, he had a disagreement with LeRoy Zider, Iowa Beef's executive vice president and chief operating officer, who ran the processing division. Zider's resignation was announced on November 18, and

Holman immediately replaced him with Steinman's lawyer son-in-law, Walter Bodenstein. Iowa Beef proclaimed in a press release that "Mr. Bodenstein's experience in meat processing and distribution in the nation's largest market, New York, will give added strength to IBP's efforts in both production and marketing." Of course, the press release didn't mention that a year earlier Judge Roberts had ruled that "Bodenstein knew virtually nothing about the meat business other than that his father-in-law took care of union leaders and meat buyers." Nor did the release quote Judge Roberts when he said, "Nothing that Bodenstein did on behalf of Cattle Pakt or C. P. Sales indicates that Steinman had abdicated his own particular responsibility . . . behind the scenes, distributing the bribe money."

As one former colleague on the Iowa Beef board observed, Holman "totally underestimated" the reaction of the financial community to his appointment of Bodenstein. The next day the New York Stock Exchange halted trading in Iowa Beef stock due to an influx of sell orders, and two days later Holman and some fellow board members were in New York huddling with officers of First National City Bank, the lead bank on its $60 million credit line. According to one good source, the bankers threatened to cut off Iowa Beef's credit line and hurl the company toward bankruptcy court unless Holman backed down. Citibank denies an overt threat, but Holman nevertheless rescinded his appointment of Bodenstein.

Iowa Beef kept its credit line. It soon after announced improved earnings and said it would begin paying cash dividends for the first time.

Nor has Holman's reputation suffered in his hometown of Sioux City. His banker there, John Van Dyke, executive vice president of the Toy National Bank, speaks for many of the people Holman depends on: "Knowing all the circumstances involved, and what a highly motivated person he is, I don't blame him at all. He wanted to get the job done and felt that that was the way to do it and he did it. He was not the kind of person to be easily deterred. Besides, what's the difference between a commission and a bribe—I don't know."

The difference, according to some estimates, amounts to retail meat prices five cents or more per pound higher— and it's the person at the supermarket checkout counter who pays.

VI

Hey, Doc!
Need a Tax Shelter?

By Stanley Penn

Jack Dick was a city slicker. He played the stock market, gambled on horses and enjoyed Manhattan's fancy restaurants. Urbane and cynical, he was the very stereotype of a New Yorker.

But Jack Dick knew his cows. Especially black, hornless Aberdeen Angus cows. Angus cows, which originated in Scotland and first came to the U.S. in the 1870s, were Dick's favorite breed. He liked them because they fatten quickly, making them cheaper to feed than some other breeds. He knew that Angus cows have big pelvic openings, often making it easier for them to calve. One day, Angus cows would help Jack Dick make a pile of money.

The Internal Revenue Code triggered Dick's interest in cows. To stimulate cattle breeding, the government turned cows into tax shelters. So it is often profitable for high-income people to invest in cattle. Like oil wells, their costs bring big tax deductions, while gains avoid much taxation. People who buy cattle for breeding purposes can deduct from their taxable income the cost of the cattle and the expense of maintaining them. A New York businessman who bought $30,000 worth of cattle in 1967 says he wrote off $20,000 in 1968 through depreciation of the animals and other deductions from income that otherwise would have been taxed at 50 percent. The government, in effect, paid

156

one-third the cost of his cows.

Thus it comes as no surprise that many well-to-do people—doctors, stockbrokers, corporate executives and movie stars—have become herd owners. This doesn't mean they buy ranches and ride the range like real cow-punchers. No, indeed. Many of these cattlepersons wouldn't know a steer from a heifer.

Instead, they buy herds from cattle breeders and pay those breeders to feed and shelter and breed them. The investors rarely, if ever, see the animals they own. When income tax time comes around, the herd owners tote up their tax deductions and the profits they may have made from the sale of the offspring that their cows produce.

Among cattle breeders, Jack Dick, who had his ups and downs as a New York promoter, became one of the biggest. When he started his cattle-breeding venture, he was broke. It didn't deter him. Using his charm and persuasive man-ner, he put together a partnership syndicate of about one hundred partners whom he induced to invest $1 million. As promoter of the venture, Dick didn't put up a nickel. With the money, he bought a 650-acre farm on behalf of the partnership at Wappinger Falls, north of New York City in Dutchess County, and stocked it with his favorite cows. There were three hundred purebred Angus and a service battery of top-grade bulls. He called the outfit Black Watch Farms.

With a team of salesmen working on handsome commis-sions, Dick corraled hundreds of other investors with promises of large tax deductions and fat profits. The inves-tors, mostly business and professional people, shelled out $3,500 for each cow (later reduced in price to $2,500), for which Black Watch Farms had originally paid about $650 to $750 each. Additionally, investors forked over $500 a cow each year (subsequently reduced to $350) as payment to Black Watch for taking care of the animals, breeding them and selling offspring for the investors' benefit.

At the outset, Black Watch Farms had great appeal. Listen to a wealthy advertising man from New York City, who bought a herd from Dick's Black Watch: "I had it all worked out. I was going to have my tax deductions, plus after five years a yearly income of $58,000 from sale of progeny, all without getting off my butt. It's a hell of a nest egg for my old age, I figured."

At its peak, Black Watch managed more than thirty thousand head of investor-owned cattle, scattered on farms and ranches in more than sixty locations in twenty states. Black Watch Farms' revenue in the fiscal year ending June 30 1969 reached nearly $30 million.

As happens in fairy tales, Dick became rich. He sold his controlling interest in Black Watch in July 1968 to the Bermec Corporation, an expansion-minded truck-leasing company whose shares were traded on the New York Stock Exchange. Dick received a pile of Bermec shares, part of which he sold for more than $5 million in cash. Then he went on a buying spree. He bought a twenty-five acre estate for $1.4 million in a posh section of Greenwich, Connecticut. The mansion, which sits at the top of Round Hill Road, had been built early in this century by the mother of Dan Topping, former owner of the New York Yankees. Dick filled the place with servants, expensive eighteenth- and nineteenth-century English paintings, antiques and art objects. He bought a Rolls Royce. He, his wife and his children lived regally.

Then it fell apart.

Many investors complained that their cows weren't producing calves at the promised rates and the calves weren't commanding the handsome prices that they'd been led to expect by Dick's salesmen. As disillusionment set in, some investors who had bought their cattle on the installment plan stopped making payments on their purchase price and also withheld payments on their maintenance contracts. Black Watch soon collapsed. A receiver appointed by the court was put in charge of the stricken company. Angry investors who had stopped making payments saw their cattle sold to slaughter houses at a fraction of their original prices to pay off creditors.

To complete the nightmarish picture, Dick was accused in civil suits in New York federal court of embezzling $3.2 million from Black Watch by forging endorsements on cashier's checks made out to suppliers and cashing the checks and using the money to pay off his personal debts. In January 1974, while the United States Attorney for the Southern District of New York was investigating the alleged embezzlement, Jack Dick died.

The collapse of Black Watch Farms was a bitter pill for many investors. It was bad enough that they had lost money on their investments. What made it worse was their belief they had been made fools of. Says a Wall Street stockbroker who was a Black Watch investor: "I needed a tax shelter and I heard cattle were a good investment. I don't know a damn thing about cattle. So I had my lawyer look into Black Watch. Everything was fine. My accountant, a brilliant guy, checked it out. The Black Watch people drove me up in a black Cadillac to their farm in Dutchess County. I saw all the certified reports. Everything checked out. And look what happened. It's a lesson."

If investors had taken a long, hard look into Dick's past, they might not have shown such eagerness to join his cattle-breeding venture. Dick had a penchant for making deals that later got him into hot water. All who knew him agree he was a smart guy, "one of the most brilliant persons I ever met," says a man who had dealings with Dick. "He would never undertake anything without making a complete study of it—cattle, paintings, anything."

But Dick had a big flaw—his belief that he was infallible. "He wouldn't listen to anyone," says a New York lawyer. "He felt he was always right." An even harsher judgment comes from a Connecticut man who disliked Dick: "He was self-destructive. Whatever he touched eventually turned to crap."

Jack Dick's misadventures began in 1952, at the age of

twenty-four, when he became a partner in his father's stove and kitchenware manufacturing business in Bayonne, New Jersey. In 1957—if his father, Sam Dick, is to be believed—Jack persuaded Sam Dick to go into semi-retirement in Florida. Later, Sam Dick returned to Bayonne to find the company insolvent, because, the father says, his son Jack signed company checks without authority and wrongfully withdrew $250,000.

Jack Dick denied all of it. "Whatever success that business had, I was responsible for." Jack Dick said he had left the firm about a year before it went under, and he blamed his father for the failure.

Jack Dick next tried to make a killing on Wall Street. In 1959, he audaciously tried to buy control of the Carpenter Steel Company (now Carpenter Technology Corporation) of Reading, Pennsylvania, whose shares were listed on the New York Stock Exchange. Lacking enough cash to do it alone, he persuaded others to join him in a joint venture: his associates put up 25 percent of the cash he needed, and Dick raised the rest through a finance company, using as collateral the Carpenter Steel stock he had bought from brokers. Dick raised about $1.5 million in this way from thirty investors.

The attempt to take over Carpenter Steel came apart. Dick's explanation was that the finance company, which has since gone out of business, misused the Carpenter Steel shares that he pledged as collateral. Dick wound up in hot water. Some of his investors sued him. Meanwhile, New York Attorney General Louis J. Lefkowitz took legal action. In a civil suit in New York Supreme Court, the attorney general charged that Dick made a false guarantee that the investors would all be protected against loss. The result was a court order permanently barring Dick from selling securities in New York. Dick consented to the order, but without conceding that he had done anything wrong.

About this time, Dick ran into trouble in yet another

stock-buying scheme. In April 1960, the Securities and Exchange Commission accused him of pretending to be somebody else in order to buy $290,000 of stock because he knew that brokerage firms wouldn't sell to him if he used his own name. The SEC got a permanent injunction in New York federal court barring Dick from any further violations of antifraud regulations.

Dick acknowledged that he had used the name of John Moritz, a friend, but with Moritz's permission, and only because he, Dick, had financial problems stemming from the Carpenter Steel fiasco.

This was a bleak period for Dick. He was being sued by investors and brokerage firms for restitution of funds that he lost through unsuccessful ventures. At the same time, he was jobless, with no money in the bank, no securities or real estate, and he was being supported by his family and his in-laws.

But he was resourceful. He started Black Watch Farms.

This was his most satisfying period. He had always wanted an outdoor life. "At fifteen, I ran away from home in New York and worked on a farm in Connecticut," he recalled. The Dicks made their home right near Black Watch Farms. Dick spent his days buying cows, supervising their breeding and selling the animals to the doctors and dentists and business people who tripped over themselves to become tax-avoiding herd owners.

To buy prize bulls, Dick made trips to Scotland, home of the Aberdeen Angus cattle. Once he paid $175,000 for an insured bull, named Lindertis Evulse, that unfortunately turned out to be sterile. But Dick wasn't defeated. He got the $175,000 back from the insurance company and then took the bull off the insurance firm's hands for a payment of $1. Then, the publicity-wise Dick had the bull operated on in an attempt to restore its fertility. Though the operation was a failure, it drew widespread newspaper coverage that helped bring attention to Dick's Black Watch Farms.

Even Dick's critics concede he helped glamorize the

161

cattle-breeding business. Would-be investors were flown to the Black Watch spread at Wappinger Falls in a twin-engine Beechcraft or driven in a big limousine. They were feted at barbecues and treated to professional entertainment. "We had a product to sell," Dick said solemnly, "and we sold it!"

Though Dick ran Black Watch, his brother-in-law, Richard Terker, took the title of general partner. Dick carefully explained, "It would not have been a contribution to the makeup of Black Watch Farms if I was advertised as general partner, so my brother-in-law accommodated me." In short, Dick wanted to keep a low profile because of his earlier financial difficulties.

Everything was going along just fine until Black Watch ran afoul of Attorney General Lefkowitz in 1963. In a civil action, the state official charged that Black Watch attempted to defraud public investors through a "false and fraudulent" offering circular that sought to raise $5 million. The circular, according to Mr. Lefkowitz, failed to disclose that nearly all the assets of Black Watch Farms were encumbered by mortgages, and that Black Watch owed $250,000 on its herds in addition to $235,000 mentioned in the circular. What's more, there was no disclosure in the circular that of $1 million in paid-in capital, $177,000 in commissions and expenses had been deducted, leaving only $823,000 for Black Watch, according to the attorney general. As a result of the attorney general's charges, Black Watch was forced to withdraw the offering.

Dick wasn't named a defendant in the attorney general's action. But the promoter couldn't keep out of trouble. In 1964, he was accused by the attorney general of engaging in a public offering of securities in Black Watch in violation of a 1960 injunction specifically barring him from selling securities in New York. Dick was slapped with a $15,000 fine.

The attorney general's actions against Mr. Dick proved to be pinpricks. By employing sales agents to peddle cows privately in the ensuing years, Black Watch Farms rapidly increased its sales. By July 1968, it looked like a prime investment opportunity for the New York-based Bermec Corporation. Dick, who earlier had bought out his brother-in-law's interests for under $500,000, sold his controlling interest in Black Watch to Bermec for a pile of Bermec stock. He sold part of his Bermec stock for more than $5 million in cash—not a paltry profit considering that he launched Black Watch seven years earlier without a nickel of his own money. All told, Bermec shelled out $30 million of its stock in exchange for the shares of Black Watch controlled by Dick and his limited partners. For Bermec, the investment turned out to be a disaster.

Just two years later, in September 1970, Black Watch ran out of money and sought protection in the bankruptcy court from creditors. In 1971, the firm was adjudged bankrupt and was completely dissolved. Bermec, meantime, was dragged down by Black Watch's financial difficulties, and a trustee was appointed by the court to put Bermec into liquidation.

What had gone wrong with Black Watch? It all looked so good on paper with handsome profits and big tax deductions assured.

The cheery promises concealed thorny problems.

First, the outfit had expanded too fast. Instead of proving beneficial, expansion sharply increased the amount of cash that Black Watch Farms needed to properly care for high-grade beef animals. Under Dick, Black Watch spent lavishly to promote itself and to entertain potential investors in Angus cattle. But the cash that came in from investors, many of whom bought their herds on the installment plan, wasn't enough to meet the firm's heavy expenses. So Black Watch was forced to go to finance companies to borrow working capital at interest rates that ran as high as 24 percent using investors' installment notes as collateral for the loans.

Meanwhile, some investors had grown disillusioned and

stopped paying off their notes. This further intensified the firm's cash squeeze. Some cattlemen who were hired by Black Watch to take care of the herds got unhappy over the uncertainty of payment and kept the animals on a bare-bones diet. Not surprisingly, this further reduced their quality. As the animals were sold, prices paid for them dropped sharply, disenchanting even more investors. All these factors—aggravated by Dick's alleged embezzlement of $3.2 million in Black Watch funds, of which Bermec had been unaware when it bought the cattle firm—combined to bring about Black Watch Farms' collapse.

Investors claim they had been given projections that the progeny from their cows would sell for at least $1,000 to $1,100 a head. They were outraged when the animals, in many cases, fetched only $450 to $500, hardly enough to offset the yearly $350 per-head maintenance fee charged by Black Watch and the 7½ percent interest payments incurred by investors who bought their herds on the fifty-two-month installment plan.

Investors say they were told their cows would breed at a 90 percent rate, or ninety calves for every one hundred cows. It didn't work that way. Dr. Edward O'Shea, a Long Island orthodontist, says he lodged a protest with Black Watch when he discovered in 1970 that his herd wasn't breeding at the 90 percent rate. Back came a letter from the company promising to supply him with enough cattle to make up the difference between the size of his herd based on a 90 percent breeding rate and its actual, smaller size.

In short, enough cows would be added to his herd to assure that Dr. O'Shea had a total of 132 animals as of August 1 1970. Alas, when Black Watch Farms went into receivership one month later, Dr. O'Shea's herd consisted of only fifty-two animals, he says. He never did find out what happened to the other eighty. If they had been sold by anyone, he never received any of the revenue that he was entitled to.

Dr. O'Shea wasn't the only physician who claimed he

got hornswoggled. A doctor who owned a $100,000 herd charged in a federal court suit in New York that Black Watch Farms took some of his best animals and sold them to pay the company's bills. A Black Watch spokesman denied it. He said that only inferior animals were culled from the herd and they were replaced with high-grade cattle.

Still another investor complained that Black Watch Farms had reported to him sales of his cattle that never took place. He displayed invoices for two animals, with their tattoo numbers, showing that they were supposedly sold for $700 each. The investor said he later found that the animals never were sold: one had died of pneumonia, the other of bloat. A third animal supposedly fetched $800. It was really sold, but only for $158.82, according to the investor. He never saw a cent from the sale, he said.

David G. Canning, who handled auction sales of Black Watch Farms' cattle in its early years, offers an insight into what went wrong. Canning says that up to about 1965, Black Watch bought high-grade cows for its investors. "But then," he says, "Black Watch Farms began mushrooming, expanding so fast they began buying in quantity without the proper checks and safeguards. The cattle they were buying were not as good, and they were spread out over wide areas and were difficult to police. Instead of getting an 85 to 90 percent calf crop (eighty-five to ninety calves for every one hundred cows), Black Watch was getting more like a 50 percent crop," Canning says.

A Staunton, Virginia, cattle breeder, Canning was unhappy about these goings-on. "I began to see what was transpiring—this was about October or November of 1965—and went up to Mr. Dick and resigned the account," he recalls.

While troubles were piling up for investors, Jack Dick still was living high. He had sold out to the Bermec Corporation and was now busily decorating his Tudor-style mansion in Greenwich, Connecticut, with paintings, bronze sculptures, ivory carvings, silver and jade. "Every room in the house was like a museum," says a New Yorker who knew Dick. A businessman who came across Dick in London in those days says: "He was buying crystal chandeliers, silver, crockery, bookcases, every conceivable kind of thing."

An art journal described Dick's eighteenth- and nineteenth-century collection of English sporting pictures as one of the most impressive in the United States. One painting, *Goldfinder*, by the distinguished English artist George Stubbs, brought $550,000, a record for its genre, in a 1974 sale at Sotheby and Company, the big English auction house. Goldfinder, an eighteenth-century racehorse, was an ancestor of Secretariat, the 1973 U.S. triple-crown winner.

Visitors still recall the big bash that Dick threw after he bought the old Topping estate in the summer of 1968. "It was the most opulent party I ever attended," says a former neighbor who is no stranger to opulent parties. "Everywhere you turned were servants in medieval costume. Most of us went out of curiosity because we'd heard about the tremendous amount of money he had." Another guest says: "The party had a kind of diplomatic flavor, with klieg lights and private guards all over the place. Most of the people seemed to be from the neighborhood, and they seemed to know each other, but nobody knew the host or hostess."

Despite his wealth, things began to go downhill for Dick. In 1969, his father, Sam Dick, got a restraining order against Jack Dick in connection with a $20 million lawsuit that the father filed against the son, claiming that Jack had reneged on an agreement. This tied up Jack Dick's assets and prevented him from paying off various creditors, including the Internal Revenue Service. The IRS said it was owed $1.5 million; State National Bank of Connecticut claimed nonpayment of a $500,000 mortgage debt, and Chase Manhattan Bank had a $477,000 claim.

Jack Dick's new-found wealth had helped to trigger the

dispute with his father. In his lawsuit, Sam Dick contended that Jack had promised, in an agreement dated August 6 1960, to split any future financial gains. Jack signed the agreement, according to his father, in appreciation for Sam Dick's help in paying off some of Jack's debts, including money owed by Jack as a result of his ill-fated stock-purchase venture in Carpenter Steel. Moreover, Sam Dick claimed, he even paid debts that son Jack owed bookies. When Jack Dick was broke in late 1959 and early 1960, the father says, he was giving his son $200 a week for living expenses.

Sam Dick says that when Jack sold out to Bermec, Jack said jubilantly, "Dad, we don't have to worry from now on. We are worth millions."

In March 1969, Sam Dick, his wife, Betty, and their other son, Eddie, went to Jack Dick's mansion in Greenwich to persuade Jack to live up to his part of the alleged agreement to share his fortune with his father. But Jack wouldn't talk to him. In fact, he wouldn't even let his family into his house. Instead, Sam Dick said in a pretrial deposition, Jack had father, mother and brother Eddie arrested by the Greenwich police for trespassing, a charge that later was dismissed.

In his own defense, Jack Dick said he got his lawyer to remove his parents and brother from his property only after they began throwing rocks at his house "and threatening to make this my burial ground."

It was then that Sam Dick began his $20 million suit against son Jack. A former Black Watch salesman says Sam Dick told him, "I've got to take care of Eddie (Jack Dick's brother). Before I die I have to see Eddie set. Why should (obscenity) Jack live like a lord in his castle when we have nothing?" The former salesman says he tried to reason with the elder Dick. "I said, 'Sam, Jack has always been giving you money. You have been living pretty good, and Jack made the wedding for Ed, and you have nothing to complain about.' Sam Dick replied, 'Never mind. I didn't get my fair share, and beside that, whatever I get, at least I will save it for Jack, because he makes it and loses it every time.'"

Jack Dick insisted that he never agreed to split his financial gains with his father. If Jack Dick is to be believed, he didn't get a penny from his father in paying off the 1959–60 damage suits against him. What's more, Jack Dick contended, he generously supported his folks and brother Eddie.

"I paid for my brother's wedding and honeymoon," Jack Dick said. "I even paid for the telegram his wife sent me saying that I'm worse than Hitler." But his folks kept nagging for more money, according to Jack. At one point, his father paid a visit to Wappinger Falls when Jack was living there and running Black Watch Farms. His father threatened that "if I didn't increase support-payments, he and Betty (Jack Dick's mother) would picket in front of Black Watch with sandwich signs, advertising for all to see that I had deserted them," Jack said. To avoid the publicity, he added, he yielded to their demands.

By 1969, according to Jack Dick, he was giving his father $5,000 a month in support payments. He said he gave other amounts too. "I bought 8,000 shares of Gateway Sporting Goods, and when I had a profit of $30,000, I gave them $7,000," Jack Dick said. A Stamford, Connecticut, judge eventually ruled against the elder Dick, declaring that the controversial agreement wasn't enforceable. Sam Dick appealed and lost.

If the father was upset by his son's actions, picture the indignation of Bermec officials when they discovered that Jack Dick neglected to mention a few things before he unloaded Black Watch Farms.

Bermec, for example, had been unaware that some purchasers of cattle had been threatening Black Watch with legal action. The buyers complained that their cows weren't turning out the number of calves promised and the offspring weren't fetching the promised prices. The upshot was that Bermec had to shell out $2.5 million to settle these investors' claims.

There was worse in store. The company apparently didn't learn until after it bought Black Watch that Dick had allegedly looted $3.2 million from Black Watch between October 1966 and June 1968, his last full month in control.

As alleged in several suits against Dick and others in New York federal court, Black Watch suppliers submitted invoices to Black Watch for the sale of cows at about $750 each. Dick assertedly submitted phony invoices that showed an inflated cost to Black Watch of $1,750 for each cow. (Investors paid $3,500 a head.) Cashier's checks were then bought at the bank where Black Watch maintained its accounts. Suppliers received cashier's checks in the amounts owed them, $750 per cow, while Dick assertedly cashed cashier's checks for the $1,000 difference between the inflated amount and the actual sales price charged Black Watch.

According to one suit, a former official of the bank endorsed some of the cashier's checks that were made payable to suppliers. These checks were allegedly cashed at the bank under the bank official's supervision. This official, who is no longer with the bank, denies any wrongdoing. He concedes that he endorsed some of the checks, but only at Dick's behest after receiving Dick's assurances that the check-cashing procedure was routine business.

"Dick used me," the ex-official says he now realizes. "He used to say to me, 'I'm your biggest customer of the bank. Take care of things for me.' I've learned a hell of a lesson. I spent four years of hell with this goddam thing, and I did it because I figured he was a good customer of the bank." The U.S. attorney for the Southern District of New York conducted an investigation, but called it off at some point after Dick's death in early 1974. No indictments were ever brought. Dick had maintained his innocence.

Swindled!

After Bermec bought Black Watch, it reduced the price of cows to investors to $2,500 each from the $3,500 charged by Black Watch under the Dick regime.

Understandably upset with Black Watch's affairs, Bermec officials took action. The company got Dick to agree to make restitution by giving Black Watch a $4.5 million promissory note for liabilities that he incurred when he ran Black Watch Farms. Unfortunately for Bermec, Dick never got around to paying off the note. The note was secured with Bermec shares owned by Dick. But the shares quickly shrank in value as Bermec came on hard times. Today, they are valueless.

Finally, the Securities and Exchange Commission took notice of Black Watch. In January 1969, after Bermec had come into control, the SEC informed Black Watch that it must register its sales programs, consisting of purchase and maintenance contracts, as a security regulated by the Securities Act of 1933. Black Watch was forced to halt the sale of cattle for three months, nearly until the end of March 1969, when the Black Watch registration statement became effective.

A Black Watch prospectus, available to the investing public, contained information that might have interested those investors who had purchased their cattle in the period before Black Watch was required to register with the SEC. Few of these earlier investors apparently saw the statement. It summed up an opinion by the SEC staff that investors who had contracted for herds before the issuance of the prospectus were entitled to rescind their purchase and get their money back.

There was no stampede, then at least, to recover the money. One investor, typical of many, indignantly complained that he wasn't aware of this option. "I never received any notice of such a right and first heard of it in the fall of 1970," said the investor, who in August 1968 had bought a $100,000 herd from Black Watch. When he found out about his rights of recovery in the fall of 1970, it was much too late to do anything. Black Watch had gone broke. If you can believe Bermec, Black Watch Farms didn't try to conceal investors' rights. Anyway, Bermec has said, it was the responsibility of the investors' lawyers and accountants to keep track of their clients' rights.

Black Watch, of course, would have gone down the drain sooner than it did if many investors had rushed to recover their investments. A few fortunate ones did get out in time. One bitter investor says he was informed that Allen Meckler, son of H. L. Meckler, the Bermec chairman, had disposed of his herd by the end of 1969. In Allen Meckler's defense, a spokesman says that Allen sold his cows well before anyone had reason to believe that Black Watch Farms was headed for disaster.

Bermec blamed the failure of Black Watch on a number of things: the 1969 recession, which may have discouraged investors from sinking money in cattle, and tight money, which certainly made it more costly for Black Watch to obtain loans for needed working capital.

Also blamed was the 1969 tax-reform bill enacted by Congress. It reduced some of the investors' tax benefits. Herd owners were now required to retain their cattle at least two years before selling the animals at capital gains rates. In the past, they had to hold the animals only one year. More significantly, a part of investors' profits from sale of their cattle now was going to be taxed at a higher rate than before. Under a complicated formula, some of these profits would be treated as ordinary income. To high-bracket investors, that meant such profits would be taxed at 50 percent. In the past, their gain generally had been taxed at only 25 percent.

The fall of Black Watch helped trigger the failure of Bermec, its parent company. The bankruptcy courts appointed trustees to sell off the companies' assets to anybody willing to purchase them. As might be expected, the investors in Black Watch herds, as well as those who bought Bermec shares on the New York Stock Exchange in the belief the company had a bright future, were bitter over what had happened to the two companies. In suits in New York federal court, they blamed the Black Watch and Bermec troubles on bad management and fraud.

Jack Dick, the one-time head of Black Watch, for example, was accused of overstating Black Watch assets, understating its earnings and falsely portraying a market for the sale of cattle at prices far higher than actually existed.

Moreover, according to some suits, Bermec officials sought to hide Black Watch's troubles in hope of hushing up a possible scandal and preventing a decline of Bermec's shares on the New York Stock Exchange. The earnings of Black Watch were consolidated with those of Bermec; thus any fall in Black Watch earnings would adversely affect Bermec.

An aggrieved Black Watch investor charged that Bermec officials put out a misleading press release in January 1970 announcing the discontinuance by Black Watch of sales of herds to investors. The reason given by Bermec was that Black Watch had "reached the optimum size for economic operations." But the real reason, according to the investor's suit, was that the SEC had refused to clear a new Black Watch prospectus in December 1969 unless Black Watch informed the public in the prospectus of its weakened condition. Without such SEC clearance, Black Watch was barred by law from selling any more herds to investors, thereby cutting into its cash flow.

"Black Watch was dying because cash flow was down," the somber investor said. "The only dependable source of cash was new victims (investors), but the SEC had foreclosed further sales."

By September 1970, Black Watch had run out of cash and sought protection against creditors from the bankruptcy court. Herd owners were alarmed. What would happen to their cattle? Was beleaguered Black Watch in any shape to feed and shelter more than 30,000 cows and bulls on farms and ranches in different parts of the country?

Hey, Doc! Need a Tax Shelter?

A bunch of unhappy investors met in a mid-town Manhattan hotel to discuss their plight. A bit of their conversation follows:

"You gonna keep the damn cows?"

"Yeah."

"Who's gonna take care of them?"

"I'll find me some cowboys."

"You think it's so easy to find cowboys?"

The problem that investors faced was that their herds were split up in ten or twenty locations in different states. It would be a time-consuming task to round up each investor's original herd. Black Watch management came up with a proposal. It offered to give each investor the same number of cows of like kind and quality from one location.

But some investors violently objected to the plan. "For one thing, how do I know I'll get the same kind of animals?" an investor grumbled. "The company's records are not in the best of shape. One month I get a record showing I have a cow with tattoo No. 15. Next month, No. 15 doesn't show up, and I have No. 18. I called up to ask, and they said the computer system wasn't working. If I transfer my cows, I want mine, not somebody else's."

Investors faced another problem. Black Watch owed nearly $1 million in fees to independent farmers and ranchers who managed some of the investor-owned herds. One indignant investor said: "How do I know the farmer hasn't attached a lien on my cattle because the company hasn't paid its bills? That farmer might have slit these animals' throats and sold my cattle for slaughter."

Harold E. Martin, of Millbrook, New York, was named receiver for Black Watch Farms. His assignment was to dispose of all the cattle or find new locations for them. He describes the magnitude of the task he faced:

"The cattle had to be fed, but Black Watch had no funds to continue their maintenance, and herd owners were not making current maintenance payments. At the same time, cattle could not be removed from locations because of the existing liens for maintenance. And there appeared to be no effective way to raise funds to discharge the liens. The vicious circle appeared to be complete." Martin adds that the books and records of Black Watch Farms were in complete disorder. There were no financial and audit controls. Security measures to protect the cattle against theft were nonexistent and Black Watch had few competent employees left to handle things.

An aide to Martin elaborates:

"Any bankruptcy is a disaster, and this was no exception. We had all these cattle, and no maintenance money to handle them. They were starving, and scattered all over. Look at the problems in disposing of them. The whole thing was a mental hernia." Compounding the problem, the aide says, was the distress of the investors, who had suffered a severe blow to their egos. "In their own fields, they are tough, aggressive and successful," says the trustee's aide. "They aren't used to losing money."

More than half of all the Black Watch investors chose to pay their bills in full and take their cattle off the receiver's hands. Many of these animals were then sold outright to farmers, or transferred by the investors to new grazing sites where ranchers, for a fee, took care of the animals. The Cross L Ranch Company of Meeker, Colorado, agreed to maintain 2,500 animals transferred from thirty-six Black Watch sites in seventeen states. Joseph H. Louis Jr., president of Cross L, says half the animals were in fine shape when he got them, but the rest were "in various states of starvation."

Other Black Watch investors decided not to keep up their payments and abandoned their animals. These cows were sold for slaughter by the receiver for about $200 a cow, a far cry from the $2,500 to $3,500 that investors had originally paid. The receiver used the proceeds from the sale of these cows to help pay off Black Watch Farms' debts.

Those investors who hadn't fully paid up their contracts

faced a bitter pill: though they had abandoned their herds, they were still obligated legally to continue paying. Many investors had signed notes to pay monthly installments. Black Watch, hard up for cash, had borrowed from commercial lenders, giving the investors' notes as collateral for the loans. As a result, these investors now found that they owed the balance not to Black Watch but to the commercial lenders, or factors.

Some of the factors, instead of demanding that the investors pay up the balance on the notes, offered to settle the debts for a payment of fifty cents on the dollar. But at least one Black Watch investor turned down the initial offer, claiming that he had already sustained a heavy loss on the cattle that he abandoned and that he was damned if he'd pay another nickel to anybody. But the factor was relentless. The investor, a Wall Street stockbroker, says, "I was getting telegrams late at night. Then one day there was a knock at my door, and my wife answered. The person who knocked said, 'Is your husband home?' 'No,' my wife said. 'I'm a good friend of his,' this person said, 'can I leave something?' This good friend was the note holder. He left me a summons."

The stockbroker owed $30,000 on his investment contract. The lender who held his note agreed to reduce his demands to something less than fifty cents on the dollar. This left the stockbroker in a quandary: should he start a suit seeking to avoid any payment, or get the note holder out of his hair by settling? The broker decided to settle.

"If I'd sued," the broker explains, "my legal expenses would have been a minimum $5,000 to $6,000. It wasn't worth it." After handing the note holder a check in settlement of his debt, the broker was informed, "you still owe me $15.52." For what? the broker wanted to know. "For out-of-pocket expenses, including the cost of serving you with the summons," the note holder politely replied.

When Black Watch went broke in September 1970, Dick emerged from seclusion. He showed up at an investors'

175

meeting at the Manhattan hotel and made an eloquent plea for their support. He promised that if they would back him with financial help, he'd make Black Watch Farms the big success it once was. This time, his charm didn't work. Too many Black Watch investors had been badly burned by past optimism, and they were reluctant to throw in more money.

Dick retreated to his mansion in Greenwich to try to think of ways to work himself out of his legal and financial morass. He was being sued by creditors and by his father; he was shortly to be sued by Black Watch investors for fraud. Then in September 1971, in a case unrelated to Black Watch Farms, Dick was hit with a forty-six count indictment, charging him with grand larceny and forgery in the theft of $840,000 from a New York money lender by using false documents to get a loan for that amount. Dick pleaded innocent. Before he could be brought to trial in New York, he died in January 1974 at the age of forty-five.

Dick will long be remembered by cattle breeders, who are of the opinion that the Black Watch scandal badly damaged an otherwise reputable industry. Breeders, together with tax attorneys and accountants, insist that cattle still provide a lucrative tax shelter for high-income investors.

But no one will persuade Dr. O'Shea, the Long Island orthodontist, of that. "I wouldn't touch a cow again with a ten-foot pole," he says. And that might serve as an epitaph for Jack Dick, the city slicker who knew his cattle.